JURY SERVICE

Alan Jones was called to the Bar in 1961. From 1962 to 1964 he was employed as a magistrates' clerk in London and Cardiff, and following this he practised as a barrister for sixteen years. He has contributed articles to the *Journal of Criminal Law* and to the *Justice of the Peace*. He has now retired and lives in Tenerife.

JURY SERVICE

A PRACTICAL GUIDE

Alan Jones

ROBERT HALE · LONDON

Copyright © Alan Jones 1983
First published in Great Britain 1983
First paperback edition 1990

Robert Hale Limited
Clerkenwell House
Clerkenwell Green
London EC1R 0HT

The right of Alan Jones to be identified as author
of this work has been asserted by him in accordance
with the Copyright, Designs and Patents Act 1988.

British Library Cataloguing in Publication Data

Jones, Alan, *1930–*
  Jury service: a practical guide.
  1. England. Criminal courts. Jury service. Procedure
  I. Title
  344.205′75

  ISBN 0–7090–4010–5

Printed in Great Britain by
St Edmundsbury Press Limited, Bury St Edmunds, Suffolk
Bound by WBC Bookbinders Limited

Contents

Preface

A buff coloured envelope through the letter-box usually brings bad news: a tax or rate demand, a gas, electricity or telephone bill. Another which causes many people concern is a notice to attend to perform jury service. It means for many great personal inconvenience but, if the existing system of criminal justice is to continue, it is an essential duty. It can also be an interesting and rewarding experience. I believe though that it would be both more rewarding to the individual juror and a duty better executed if the juror knew more of what was going on at the criminal trial and more about his part in it from the beginning. I have referred to the criminal trial as, with the rarest exceptions, juries are no longer used in civil cases in England, so rarely as to be of no practical importance. There is one other type of jury, that is a Coroner's jury which decides the cause of death at an inquest: the procedure there is completely different and I do not intend to deal with it. It is also important to realize that the system of criminal trial in Scotland has many differences from that in England, but, perhaps, whilst not being applicable in detail, a Scottish juror may find much of interest in this book.

This book is not a guide to the location of courts or to the allowances and facilities on all these matters, and court officers are usually very helpful in dealing with queries. It is, however, intended to help the juror know what is going on in court, especially when he has been excluded from the court which happens from time to time (see Chapter 5), from the time the case starts until the end. This is necessary as the courts do not tell jurors what is going on all the time, sometimes from oversight, sometimes deliberately.

As far back as the middle of the eighteenth century, Serjeant Davey (in those days senior barristers were known as Serjeants or Serjeants-at-Law) said, when addressing a jury. 'You gentlemen who are on the outside of the curtain do not see the tricks and management within; we that are on the inside see the whole.'

This book is an attempt to draw back the curtain.

1

Selection and Attendance: Not Being a Juror

Liability for jury service is now governed by the Juries Act 1974. I am not going to suffocate the reader with legal references; if he wants Act and section he will find them in books such as *Archbold's Criminal Pleading, Evidence and Practice*. The Act provides that all persons between the ages of eighteen and sixty-five are liable for jury service, providing that their names are on the electoral roll, and subject to a fairly long list of exemptions, such as lawyers, clergymen, police and prison officers, members of parliament, military and naval personnel, the mentally ill and others. If you are in one of the exempt categories you will almost certainly know but if you are in any doubt the Crown Court will tell you. If you are in one of the exempt categories you will not be liable at any time. However, if you receive a summons to attend and you are in one of the exempt categories, do not ignore the summons but get in touch with the Crown Court. If you are not exempt you have to attend but the Crown Court has the discretion of excusing your attendance at any particular time and they are very reasonable and helpful about that. It may be some relief to jurors to know that they will receive allowances for travelling and subsistence and for financial loss, such as loss of earnings or benefits under the national insurance and social security schemes. The amounts are laid down in regulations and details can be obtained from the Crown Court.

If you receive a summons to attend for jury service on a particular date and it is difficult or inconvenient for you to attend on that date write immediately to the Crown Court concerned, or visit the court, asking to be excused on that date, with your reasons: such applications are frequently received and relate to such matters as the juror running a one-man business, sitting examinations or having booked and paid for a holiday at that time. In fact the Crown Court will usually excuse attendance for any sensible reason but this does not excuse attendance at a later date. In practice none of this causes much difficulty either to the juror or to the court but, occasionally, problems do arise. First, there is the juror who is legally eligible and who has no ground for not being available on a particular date but is unable to read – in which event he would not be reading this – which in a case involving documentary evidence would obviously be inappropriate, although in some cases illiteracy might prove no obstacle. Secondly, there are defects which affect ability to sit as a juror such as being blind or deaf: I can not imagine any court not excusing a person from jury service who was either blind or deaf. Most of these situations are dealt with by the officers of the Crown Court out of court so that nothing is said about them in public. How does the court know that a person who claims illiteracy or deafness is telling the truth? It receives few representations on these grounds and generally accepts the word of the potential juror. In doubt the court could ask for evidence of, say, deafness by way of a medical certificate.

There are also reasons why one should not serve on a particular jury even if eligible and without any reasonable excuse for evading jury service in general. The first that springs to mind is where the juror knows the defendant and it is quite surprising how often that happens. Consider the position in which you would find yourself as a juror with a defendant whom you knew. If you knew him and didn't like him you might find it difficult not to be prejudiced against him and he might suffer unfairly: if he knew that you didn't like him the situation would be terminated rapidly by you being challenged off the jury, of which more later. If you knew him and liked him, or even if you were indifferent in your feelings towards him, you would almost certainly feel embarrassed in judging him, particularly when his guilt might appear obvious during the course of the case. So it is best if you know a defendant to speak up when you are called into the jury box and you will be excused, thus avoiding possible injustice or embarrassment, or both! You might find the situation only a little less difficult if you know the family and, again, the best thing to do is to speak up.

Another reason which might lead to a juror withdrawing from a case is knowing a witness. One of the practical problems here is that there is no way, other than chance, in which a juror can know who the witnesses will be in a case until after he has been sworn as a juror, except that some judges, particularly in long cases, have the names and addresses of prosecution witnesses read to jurors so that if they know any of them they can say so. This helps but does not always solve the problem as a juror may know a witness, such as a fellow worker, without knowing his full name and address and, as a result, only realize that he knows a witness when he sees him: this is perhaps a problem which can not be solved in its entirety. Of course it might, in some cases, not matter whether or not a juror knows a witness, only if the defendant is disputing that witness's evidence, which would mean that you would have

11

to decide whether you accept the defendant's or the witness's version. Again, though, speak up and the Judge and Defence and Prosecution Counsel will discuss the matter. It would clearly be undesirable for you to sit on a jury and have to decide between the version given by a police officer whom you knew well and a defendant of whom you knew nothing: right or wrong, the defendant would always have a feeling of injustice, if he knew. Out of order, but perhaps best mentioned here is, 'What do you do if half-way through the prosecution case a witness is called whom you know but had not earlier known was going to be called?' The answer is simple, tell the Judge. In some cases this might result in the trial being abandoned and the case having to start again before a fresh jury, but that is a decision for the Judge; all you have to do is to be completely open about it and speak up.

A third situation which sometimes arises is where the defendant is charged with, for example, stealing property from a juror's employer, say British Rail or British Steel, although the juror may have no knowledge of the matter as a result of his employment, nor know the witnesses being called who work for his employer. However, if you are called to serve on a jury to try a defendant charged with stealing your employer's property it would be best if you mentioned that fact to the Judge in court before you take the oath.

I have mentioned the one-man business and the general preparedness of the Crown Court to release people in this position and especially so when cases are expected to last a long time. Most people will have read of cases going on for months, but even those which last for weeks only, apart from the strain of the case, can cause great problems for the small business man. I have a sneaking suspicion that, when a case is known to be likely to be a long one, jurors have put forward specious and untruthful reasons for not being able to sit on that case. It would be very difficult to prove that a juror was not telling the truth when he said that he knew that defendant. It is something we will never know; but fortunately for the system, a combination of the responsible attitude by most potential jurors and the sensible attitude of most court officials makes it very doubtful that such malpractice amounts to much.

2
Swearing the Jury: Challenges

You have arrived at the Crown Court for jury service and have either no valid reason not to perform the duty or, perhaps, your request to be excused has been rejected. What now? Arrangements vary, particularly according to the size of the court complex, some have a dozen or more court-rooms whilst others have only one or two, but generally you will be directed to a jury assembly room and in due course you will be led by a court usher into one of the court-rooms. It is usual before that is done for a court official to give you a short talk on some of the practical details of your task. Once in the court-room you will be directed to sit in seats at the rear of the court. At this stage all you are likely to see is the Judge on the Bench, with a court official in front of him, and the backs of the heads of the barristers, solicitors and the defendant. The court official, frequently referred to as the Associate, a hangover from the old Assize Court days, or more correctly as the Clerk, will have a small bundle of cards in a box and will draw the cards from it one at a time, each time calling a name, twelve in all. This procedure is carried out to ensure that the selection of the jury is a random one and that there has been no 'fixing' of the membership of the jury, unlikely as that would in any event be. So, in turn, twelve of you file into the jury box and the swearing of the jury begins. However, like almost everything else in a court, that is not as simple as it sounds: but let us first consider what happens when there are no interruptions, objections, challenges or other problems.

You will all be asked to stand and told that when you have taken the oath you should sit down. The Clerk will say to each of the twelve, individually, words to the effect, 'Take the Testament in your right hand and read the words on the card aloud.' Most people do just that, perhaps a little nervously and on occasion general embarrassment is caused by a juror with a stammer or by a juror who cannot read from the card, sometimes because he has forgotten his spectacles. Of more importance is what is not said to the juror. He is not told, for example, that if he is of the Jewish faith that he can take the oath on the Old Testament and cover his head, although in fact most Jewish jurors would know that. Of more importance in practice is that the juror is not told in open court that he may affirm instead of swearing on oath. The battle over oaths and affirmations took place in the last century with Charles Bradlaugh being refused leave to take his seat in the House of Commons without taking an oath. He was expelled and the electors of Northampton, in 1882, re-elected him: that time he was allowed to take his seat without taking an oath. In 1888 the Oaths Act was passed allowing a juror or witness to affirm, but only if he stated that to swear an oath was inconsistent with his religious beliefs or that he had no religious belief: for a long time, having to declare publicly that one had no religious belief was sufficient discouragement to people affirming, resulting in oaths being taken which were meaningless, although legally valid. Now every adult has the right to affirm, juror, witness, defendant. Occasionally a juror does elect to affirm and if he is one of the first it is noticeable that his example is frequently followed by others. It would be a good idea if jurors were told, in open court, that they can take an oath or affirm and, in Wales, either in English or Welsh. This then is what happens when all goes smoothly: let us see now what can prevent the smooth flow – under three headings.

The first has already been dealt with in outline, where the juror has some good reason for not being a juror, such as relationship or friendship with the defendant or a witness in the case. This, in any event, is a matter within the knowledge of both the juror and the defendant and requires little further comment. The other two headings are different: challenges to jurors by the defence and the prosecution.

Whilst a jury has only twelve members, as many as twenty of the panel of jurors have been brought into court. The jury panel may be of any number depending upon the number of courts sitting at the Crown Court centre: a centre with two courts might have a jury panel of, say, thirty-five, whilst a centre with ten courts may have some one hundred and fifty potential jurors. It is necessary to have some spare potential jurors as objection may be made to individual jurors by both the defendant and the prosecution, although nowadays on a much more restricted scale than formerly. Taking the defendant first: until 1977 he could object to any seven jurors without giving any reason. He might, for instance, not like the look of a juror; he might not want to have people from ethnic minorities or women on the jury; or it might have been more at the instigation of his barrister, who has objected to give the defendant the impression that he was really fighting his case. The number was reduced to three in 1977, whether to restrict the number of challenges or to save money by reducing the size of jury panels is not clear. Now, however, the right to challenge 'without cause' has been abolished.

The defendant still has the right to challenge 'for cause', that is to say, by advancing some valid reason why the juror should not serve. The possibilities for objection are theoretically without limit, but in reality occur rarely. Often the juror has disqualified himself by declaring his knowledge of a defendant or a key witness in a case and I have never encountered a single case of a challenge 'without cause'. It could be argued that with the right to challenge 'without cause' it was not necessary to give a reason, but I doubt this as I never encountered a valid reason, other than a subjective one in the mind of the defendant, for objecting to a juror.

The Prosecution also has the right to object to jurors: this is likely to be due to the juror having criminal convictions, although this is very rare as the juror in question will usually have been vetted-out by the Crown Court officers as ineligible. If the Prosecution finds itself in the position where it cannot challenge 'for cause' – perhaps the juror has no criminal convictions but is an associate of criminals – then the Prosecution can ask for him to 'Stand by for the Crown', which means that he will not be sworn unless it is impossible to swear a jury because the jury panel has been exhausted: this is so unlikely that I doubt if the reader will ever encounter it.

I cannot leave the subject of challenges without referring to a practical difficulty which used to arise often, although now a rarity. This arises from the layout of most of our courts. The defendant sits in the dock, usually accompanied by two prison officers, in front of him sits his solicitor or the solicitor's clerk and in front of him the barrister. It would be difficult to imagine and design a system more conducive to the breakdown of communication between a defendant and his lawyers. It has frequently occurred that between the time the Clerk of Court has called a juror's name and the defendant's barrister has uttered the magic word 'object', the juror has started to be sworn. This situation led to one pedantic Judge rejecting the challenge and the juror being sworn. The defendant appealed to the Court of Appeal, which took a robust view and said that 'sworn' meant 'being sworn', thus upholding the conviction of a patently guilty man. The court did, however, say that the Judge had a discretion to allow the challenge. This problem of communication between barrister and defendant is made difficult, in all situations, because of the interposing of the solicitor in the chain of communication. Why, in normal cases, is the defendant not situated next to his lawyers, as in the United States courts? It can only be put down to the barrister's desire, perhaps understandable in many cases, not to have too much to do with his client!

Eventually the jury is sworn, all twelve. Although I have dealt with a number of problems it is surprising how smoothly the whole procedure usually runs. Like many barristers, I have thought what would happen if a potential juror were to refuse to take the oath or affirm, giving as his reasons that he did not believe in the criminal law or had some prejudices which would make it inappropriate for him to sit as a juror in any case. I think either he would be asked to stand by for the Crown or the Judge would quietly tell him to go away, but there are judges who would inflate the incident into a *cause célèbre*. We are lucky though that the typical juror takes a responsible attitude towards his duties, the others are, perhaps, overawed into conforming.

JURY SERVICE

3

The Court and its Participants

Most men and women when they enter the court as potential jurors are going into a court for the first time, or at least into a Crown Court for the first time, and naturally are keen to get their bearings and to identify the others taking part in the case, or at least those who are in court. The Judge is easy to identify but what about the man, or woman, sitting in front of him in a robe with a wing collar and bands (the name given to the two pieces of linen hanging down in front), who, if the Judge is a High Court Judge will be wearing a wig: otherwise he doesn't! Then the barristers, but what of the people sitting behind them? Solicitors or their clerks. Remember this about everyone who is taking part in the trial, Judge, barristers, solicitors, everyone – like human beings in general, some are outstanding whilst others are frankly appalling with all possible intermediate standards. I am not sure which is the more embarrassing, a poor Judge and good counsel or vice versa. On the whole though we are fortunate in that the standard is as high as anywhere else in the world and higher than in the majority of countries: perhaps the errors are as much due to off-days as to ability, but remember, as a juror, that the same comments can be made about members of a jury.

Let us start with the Judge, and this is not quite as straightforward as you might have expected. If the Judge is wearing a scarlet robe he will be a High Court Judge and will be known as Mr Justice —— and will be addressed as My Lord and referred to as Your Lordship. He will have been a barrister of many years' standing and experience and more often than not a Queen's Counsel, of which more later, for some years before becoming a High Court Judge. If he is not wearing a scarlet robe but a dark robe with violet edging and a scarlet sash from shoulder to waist, he will be a Circuit Judge. He will be known as His Honour Judge —— and addressed and referred to as Your Honour: he will nearly always be a barrister of long standing, many have been Queen's Counsel, but a steadily increasing number have been solicitors before going on to the Bench. High Court and Circuit Judges differ, amongst other things, in that the former are fewer in number, are treated with greater respect and are better paid than the latter: the former are not necessarily better Judges. In addition High Court Judges (sometimes referred to as 'Red Judges' when they try criminal cases and wear their scarlet robes) are London based and visit provincial Crown Courts all over the country whilst Circuit Judges are locally based and usually sit at courts in the area in which they are based. One important difference is that High Court Judges are intended to try the more important and difficult cases, in fact cases such as treason and murder can only be tried by them. In practice Circuit Judges frequently find themselves trying long and difficult cases, the sort you read about in the newspapers as lasting for months. The marked reluctance of some High Court Judges to try these long cases has on occasion caused comment amongst lawyers.

The Judge though may wear neither a scarlet gown nor a scarlet sash, in which case he will be either a barrister or solicitor sitting as a part-time Judge, known either as a

Recorder or Deputy Circuit Judge and will also be addressed as Your Honour. A Recorder commits himself to sit for not less than twenty days a year whilst a Deputy Circuit Judge does not have to do so. The object of this system is both to provide experience for lawyers before they are selected for appointment to the Bench and also to provide a flexible reserve of judicial manpower. It has been said that it is a cheaper way of running courts, but I doubt that this is a prime motive. So your part-time Judge may be a Queen's Counsel, a junior barrister or a solicitor, but whether he be a full-time Judge, High Court or Circuit, or a part-time Judge, he carries out the same function and I will refer to him from now on simply as the Judge.

If the Judge is a High Court Judge you will see one other person on the Bench with him and you may well see two or three others there from time to time. The one you will definitely see is the Judge's Clerk, who travels round with the High Court Judge wherever he goes and carries out administrative functions such as seeing that the Judge's papers are in court. One of the functions he carries out in court, which is another hangover from the old Assize courts, is that when the jury has been sworn, the Clerk of Court will call out the names of the jury whilst the Judge's clerk will count them. When he has done this he will say, 'Members of the Jury, are you all sworn?' No answer is expected and rarely is one given. This procedure is not followed with other Judges as they do not have clerks of their own: there seems no logical reason for this to continue. Particularly on the first day of his sitting at a Crown Court, a High Court Judge is often accompanied by such local dignitaries as the Lord Lieutenant of the County (wearing a dark blue military uniform), the High Sheriff (usually in a black velvet suit with breeches and lace at the collar and cuffs) and a clergyman known as the Judge's chaplain. When there was the death penalty for murder, after the Judge had pronounced sentence the Chaplain said "Amen". None of these people have any significance or connection with the conduct of the trial and are further hangovers of the old Assize Court system.

In front of the Judge will be the Clerk of the Court who will rarely be, nor need be, legally qualified. His knowledge of what is happening will vary very considerably with experience some have little more knowledge than is necessary for them to carry out the fairly formal tasks they have in court, others fully understand all that is going on. His tasks, in so far as you will witness them, are reading the charges to the defendant, and repeating them to you, swearing witnesses and, at the end of the case, asking the jury for its verdict. He has many other administrative tasks which are essential to the proper running of the court, one of which you may see him getting on with while the case is proceeding.

You may notice that the Clerk has a number of files in front of him which will either be in respect of future trials, to ensure that they are ready to proceed, or relating to trials which have been concluded. His task regarding the concluded trials is to 'tax' the costs. 'Tax' has nothing to do with the general concept of taxation but is a legal term used to describe the process of deciding how much the lawyers, barristers and solicitors in a case are to be paid. Whilst a defendant who is paying for his defence agrees with his solicitor how much he will pay, he is the rarity in the criminal courts. The vast majority of defendants are legally aided and in those cases the Court decides the proper amount of remuneration for the lawyers. The same system is applied in respect of the lawyers' fees for the prosecution. The result, surprisingly, is that in nearly all cases the lawyers do not know how much they are going to be paid until the cases are over! They put in written representations as to the time taken in preparation, conferences and other activities such as viewing the scene of the crime, whilst the Clerk of Court has full details as to the time spent in court on the case. It is then his task to try and arrive at a fair figure. Arguments over the amount of fees sometimes attract as much interest amongst the lawyers as the cases themselves. Clerks of Court have a difficult task as they are conscious that they are dealing with public money and, on the whole, are, rightly, very suspicious of the length of time claimed by many lawyers as having been spent on preparation. There are two problems here. One genuine, the other not so. A very slow, not so astute lawyer, may spend ten hours on preparation whilst a quick, experienced lawyer may only need two or three hours on the same task. Do you pay the one, say, £200, and the other £20 or £30? The second problem is the false inflation of preparation time by lawyers to attempt to get the fees to which they think they are entitled. These problems are almost insoluble. Much could be done to prevent the second if any lawyer who accepts cases which have to be 'taxed' was made to keep an exact record of the times he devotes to each case, in diary form with date and times. Then if there is any query his claims can be checked against all his cases in the year. I doubt if this would ever be necessary as the very existence of this record would marvellously reduce the claims for preparation time, and much public money would be saved. If this seems a digression it might not be unhelpful for the juror to be aware of the background atmosphere which often exists.

The other person in front of the Judge will be the official shorthand writer. You may be surprised to learn that he, or she, is not employed by the Crown Court and is not a civil servant. Shorthand writers are employed by private firms who submit tenders to the Lord Chancellor's Department (the department responsible for the running of the Crown Courts) to provide shorthand writers at specific courts.

This system originated in the old Assize and Quarter Sessions Courts which did not sit continuously but for fairly short periods, at intervals, so that it would have been uneconomic to have employed full-time shorthand writers. To try now to change the system would not be easy, even if it would be worthwhile, and to obtain sufficient competent shorthand writers would be very difficult.

You will note that some shorthand writers take the evidence down manually whilst others use special shorthand machines. Their notes are principally needed when a defendant has been convicted and wishes to appeal to the Court of Appeal. Sometimes such an appeal needs the whole of the shorthand note to be transcribed, sometimes only part of it. It is the sheer bulk of work which has to go into those transcripts which is as often as not the cause of long delays in appeals being heard. You may also see that some shorthand writers have cassette recorders as well; these are for their own use, but a number of experiments have been made with recording the proceedings officially in this way. Whether that method will be adopted remains to be seen, but one difficulty would be that when, during the case, a dispute arises over what a witness said, it would be very difficult to check, whilst at present the shorthand writer can be asked to check his notes. Most of these shorthand writers are excellent, some less so, chiefly because of the great increase in the number of courts in recent years: it should never be forgotten that to record a note of what is being said by several people in rotation is very difficult and when you realize that the shorthand writer is expected to do this for as long as two and a half hours without a break, as a matter of course, it is astonishing that such good records are kept. Fortunately it is unlikely that an experience one Court of Quarter Sessions had some years ago will be repeated. For some months a lady sat in the usual place and assiduously took notes, or so it appeared. Then a transcript was required and it transpired that she had no knowledge of shorthand and had spent months scribbling what looked like Sanskrit, which looks not unlike shorthand to the untrained eye!

There are two other classes of people in court who I must deal with before the lawyers. First, the prison officers who sit with the defendant in the dock. You will notice that when the defendant goes to the witness-box he will be accompanied by a prison officer: if he is accompanied by two you will know that he is considered a security risk, and most likely has a long record of violence, or that the charges against him are of the utmost gravity. What does often seem a waste of public money is the presence of two prison officers in the dock with a defendant who has no previous convictions and who faces a charge on which he will not go to prison if convicted. The other group consists of the ushers, men and women, who you will first have encountered when you arrive at court. They will direct you to the jury room when you arrive and lead you to the courtroom. In court they will bring the witnesses in and be responsible for handing around exhibits. You will generally find them helpful but one wonders how the courts used to manage without them and, also, why there are so many of them.

The lawyers in court are barristers and solicitors. The basic difference, so far as we are concerned in a criminal trial in the Crown Court, is that the barrister conducts the case, asks the questions, makes the speeches and argues points of law before the Judge, whilst the solicitor is responsible for preparing the evidence which the barrister can call and all the details which the barrister needs. In an ordinary straightforward case, for example a charge of shop-lifting, you will see two barristers, one prosecuting, one defending: if in addition you see one in a very white wig who sits there taking a note only he will almost certainly be a pupil of one of the barristers, that is to say a recently qualified barrister who is getting practical experience of court. If there are a number of defendants then each may be separately represented: this is quite understandable but, even where there is only one defendant, you may find that there are two barristers for the prosecution and two for the defence. You will always find this in murder cases and in many other long and difficult trials. Normally one on each side will be a Queen's Counsel and the other a junior barrister. A Queen's Counsel, also known as a 'Silk' from the cloth of the gown which he wears, or as leading counsel, is a barrister of long experience who has been granted a Royal Patent and who, usually, only appears in court with a junior barrister to assist him. The idea is that Queen's Counsel can concentrate on fewer, more difficult cases which the junior barrister would be unable to do. But reality and theory do not always coincide. It can occur that where there are two counsel, either for the prosecution or the defence, that both of them are junior barristers: this is sometimes caused by courts which, in legal aid cases, are responsible for granting permission to employ two counsel only if they are two junior counsel, thus saving money on lawyers' fees, as Queen's Counsel are paid as much as twice junior barristers. Also, you may find one barrister defending more than one defendant; this is also encouraged by the courts as it saves money, but it is not always possible as different defendants may have different defences, as where one defendant may be blaming the other.

You may also notice that in a long case various barristers disappear for days at a time and rather younger ones 'sit in' for them: this enables the original barrister to go off and do other cases! Needless to say, this is done because it is financially rewarding. What happens is this: the junior barrister is in court on the first day, he will also have been fully involved in the preparation of the case, and will receive the brief fee, which in a big case could easily be £3,000, and then attends for fifteen of the thirty days the case lasts, being paid 'refreshers' of, say, £100 per day, making a total of £4,500. Of course, the 'sitting in' barrister will be paid for the other days. On the face of it the original barrister will have lost £1,500 by his absence but will undoubtedly have earned much more in doing other cases, so that is a quite understandable course of action, a barrister should only do this if his client agrees: in fact, the client is often not asked and even if he is, he is unlikely to object, he is after all in a very strange situation. The only satisfactory course will be for this practice to cease; in that way one can be certain that there will be no detriment to a defendant. In a long case you may notice leading counsel turning to his junior to check what was said earlier in the case only to find that on the day that piece of evidence was given his junior had not been there and is unable to be of much assistance. The rule should be clear, once a barrister starts a case he should stay till the end.

It is an accepted fact at the Bar that the presence of a Queen's Counsel in a case usually results in the case being lengthened. This may, in part, be unfair as the cases in which QCs are briefed should be the more difficult and, consequently, longer ones, but when you have a class of lawyer who is intended to be available for long cases he has the time to spend on the case and, in some instances, no other case to go on to when the existing one is over. One factor which does exist in some cases is that if a case lasts a long time it apparently becomes classified as difficult and the bases of remuneration are inflated. It would be unjust not to say that these criticisms, whilst they are frequently correct, do not refer to all cases, nor to all barristers: many

31

are notable for their ability to clarify and shorten issues, but they are usually the busier members of the Bar.

Prior to a defendant standing trial at the Crown Court there has to be a hearing at a Magistrates' Court. Originally all the witnesses were called there to give evidence on oath and were liable to be cross-examined, and the defendant was only committed for trial if the magistrates were satisfied that he had a case to answer, not that they were of the opinion that he was guilty but simply that an explanation was called for. This was a very expensive and time-consuming exercise, and with the increase in crime was blocking the Magistrates' Courts, so a reform was introduced in the Criminal Justice Act, 1967, whereby the defendant, or his solicitor, is given copies of the prosecution statements and, if the defendant does not wish to contest the matter at that stage, he is sent for trial to the Crown Court after a very short formal hearing. If he wishes he can insist on a hearing before the magistrates (also known as the justices from their designation as justices of the peace or JPs) in the old form, or partially so, but that is not done very frequently. The important thing is that the defendant knows long before he comes to trial at the Crown Court what the case against him is and the first thing he will normally do is to obtain the services of a solicitor. A member of the public who requires legal help has to go, in the first place, to a solicitor; he can not go directly to a barrister: if necessary a solicitor will brief a barrister on behalf of the defendant, which will always be necessary in a Crown Court trial, unless the defendant decides to defend himself. In most cases in the Crown Court the defendant will be legally aided; in other words, the State will pay for his defence but, depending on his financial position, he may be called upon to make a contribution towards the cost of his defence.

Armed with the prosecution statements, the solicitor will

go through the evidence with the defendant to see how much of it he agrees with and how much he disputes and to get from him his version of what happened. This can take a long time and the complete preparation of a case can involve obtaining experts' evidence, medical, scientific or engineering, and tracing witnesses and taking statements from them. Then all this material – prosecution statements, the defendant's own version and the statements of defence witnesses as well as copies of any documents put in by the prosecution (known as exhibits) – is sent by the solicitor to the barrister in advance of the trial. This enables him to have an opportunity to consider the whole of the case and to have a conference with the defendant, at which the solicitor will be present (a barrister should never see a defendant on his own save in emergency), so as to advise the defendant, first, on his plea, guilty or not guilty. The word 'advise' is important: the barrister or solicitor can not tell a defendant what his plea is to be, that is the defendant's decision alone, but the advice can be put strongly. It is a dangerous business, as most barristers know, as there have been many cases where no apparent defence exists, or is so highly unlikely that conviction seems inevitable, but the defendant insists on his innocence and the jury has acquitted.

One situation which you are unlikely to know exists is where the defence has been properly prepared but where at the last minute the barrister is unable to conduct the defence because another case in which he has been concerned lasts longer than expected, and then the brief has to be transferred to another barrister. Everyone tries to avoid this and in many cases defendants do not object to it happening. It is very rare in the longer or more difficult cases. It is however undesirable, and little difficulty would be caused if, when this situation occurs at the last moment, a defendant should be able to have his case postponed (on one occasion at least) and a fresh date fixed when the selected barrister would be available and under a duty to be so available.

As a juror you are only concerned with cases where a defendant pleads not guilty; three things are required for a defence to run smoothly: a defendant who gives proper instructions to his solicitor, a solicitor who takes those instructions and prepares the defence properly, and a barrister who reads the brief sent to him well in advance. These three prerequisites do not always exist together but it is difficult, if not impossible, for the outsider to know which one is missing. I have seen some where all three were missing! The major problem is often that the defendant, who may well be an inadequate person, who cannot give coherent instructions, or gives ones which are impossible, very often because he is guilty and cannot think up a good story.

Less often, but not infrequently, it is poor preparation by solicitors. I have seen the following: 'Counsel will find the enclosed: prosecution statements, defendant's comments and statement which are self-explanatory.' If they were self-explanatory it might be enough but they rarely are self-explanatory. Instructions to counsel of this type are often the result of solicitors finding it almost impossible to get sensible information from the defendant. Another factor is that solicitors are lawyers, passing difficult examinations and having to spend a considerable period in a solicitor's office before being admitted as solicitors. One of the difficulties, though, in criminal cases is that in the main solicitors' training is not designed to deal with crime and they only gain this experience in practice: the result is that many firms of solicitors are not competent to deal with criminal cases and, to do them justice, many will pass criminal cases on, with the defendant's consent, to firms that are better experienced in that field. One other problem is that a firm which has a reputation for criminal defence work (by the very nature of the work the reputation must be one amongst the criminal section of society) often has too much work for the solicitors in the firm, so that defendants are passed on to articled clerks (trainee solicitors) or other staff employed by the firm. Many of these are very competent but the cases are not being handled by solicitors: it is rather like going to a doctor and being treated by a medical orderly and paying doctor's fees. Perhaps as hardly anyone is paying for his own defence nowadays it is understandable that solicitors operate this system. Not only may the person who prepared the case for counsel not be a solicitor but a clerk, articled, experienced, competent, or otherwise, but the person sitting behind counsel in court may not even be the person who prepared the case and who is familiar with it.

I am stressing this arrangement as during the course of the trial you may well hear Defence Counsel say to the Judge, 'I will take instructions, your Honour.' Despite the preparation, however good it may be, a point may arise of which the defence had no forewarning, so counsel wishes to find out what the defendant says about the matter. Counsel will then look, hopefully, at the person sitting behind him to find out the answer: he will almost certainly have to ask the defendant. The difficulty is that where that person is not conversant with the case he may well not appreciate the significance of the information required. You may observe, on occasion, a look of blank incomprehension when counsel turns to his instructing 'solicitor'. It should be made a requirement when public funds are being utilized to pay for the defence of an accused person that the solicitors who undertake the defence should allocate staff to that case who stay with it from beginning to end, in the same way, it is suggested, that counsel should not leave a case.

Jury Service

I have mentioned judges, lawyers and others in court and I have not avoided criticizing them. There is one other group to which I have not referred, the jurors. Since most of the other people in court have to perform a part which we all witness it is easy to criticize them – the Judge who cannot control his court, the lawyer who cannot stop talking – but the jury say nothing until at the end the foreman (see Chapter 13) says 'Guilty' or 'Not Guilty', so we are not in a position to comment much on them. But remember in your dealings with the other eleven members of the jury that they will differ by way of sex, age, education, occupation, intelligence, sense of responsibility, state of health and in a dozen other ways. Be patient in conversation and discussion. Remember it might appear clear to an accountant how a company's balance sheet is drawn up but the lorry driver who cannot follow it may well be in the reverse position when the question is of a lock when braking an articulated lorry. It is this wide range of experience that, in part, justifies our jury system.

4

The Opening

The Judge, the lawyers and the defendant know what the case is all about, what the defendant is charged with and the evidence that the prosecution proposes to call to establish the guilt of the defendant. At this stage you, as a juror, know nothing unless you have been in court when the indictment, that is the list of charges, was put to the defendant. Often the pleas to the indictment are taken in the absence of the jury: this is usually because the defendant has pleaded guilty to some charges but not to others and it is not considered proper for the jury to hear that he has pleaded guilty to anything. This, as you will see later, is really nonsense as you will be able to work out for yourself if the defendant has any previous convictions without a word being said about them. Perhaps the defendant faced, say, ten charges of burglary and has pleaded guilty to those where he cannot think up a defence but not guilty where he has been able to. Another case is where the defendant is charged with two offences arising out of one act, for example murder and manslaughter, and pleads guilty to manslaughter but not to murder, but later this is bound to be brought into the open. So, if you do not hear the defendant pleading to the indictment it is very likely due to one of those two sort of situations: in any event there is most likely something you should not know!

Whether or not you have heard the defendant enter his pleas, as soon as the Jury has been sworn the Clerk of Court will read the charges to you and, at the end of that, say something to the effect, 'to those charges the defendant has pleaded not guilty and it is your task to say whether he is guilty or not guilty.' All well and good when one defendant is charged with one or two straightforward charges, but when you are faced with three or more defendants who are accused of as many as twenty charges between them, the reading of the charges, without explanations, sometimes at great speed, is generally a ludicrous waste of time as no jury can possibly follow their import. Many sensible judges and Prosecuting Counsel see that juries have copies of the indictment before it is read to them: this is better than nothing but it is only historically induced lethargy which perpetuates such procedures. Having a copy of the indictment, is however, necessary at the next stage when Prosecuting Counsel is opening the case to you. If you are not given copies of the indictment ask for them: you are the real judges in the case, as you will eventually be told by the Judge.

Perhaps the best way to understand what happens next in the trial is to follow, in outline, the opening of a simple case. You are seated in the jury box, having just heard that the defendant has pleaded not guilty to burglary and theft of £10. You are expectant, the defendant nervous and apprehensive, counsel are rustling their papers and trying to look unconcerned when the Judge says, 'Yes, Mr Smith' to Prosecuting Counsel, to indicate that he may start. He will rise, bow to the Judge, and to you, and start, 'May it please Your Honour (remember in a simple case like this it would be tried before a Circuit Judge or one of the part-time judges), Members of the Jury. In this case I appear to prosecute and my learned friend, Mr John Brown, appears for the defence.' One of the things you will notice is the number of times that counsel say 'Members of the Jury', or 'Ladies and Gentlemen of the Jury', but don't spend your time counting them, interesting as that may be, as you would then miss many more interesting events.

The pattern of the opening will usually be for Prosecuting Counsel to explain the charge or charges to you that the defendant faces, telling you carefully that, although he is dealing with the law, you will take your directions on the law from the Judge, and then go on to outline the facts on which the prosecution will rely to prove its case. There are variations on this pattern as some counsel prefer to tell you the facts and then relate them to the charges which the defendant faces. In shortened, very much shortened, form the opening may sound like this:

The defendant is charged with burglary, that is entering a house, without authority, and stealing in that house £10 from the electricity meter. He used to live next door to the house broken into and a neighbour, who knows him, saw him going into the house at about 3 o'clock in the afternoon. When the householder returned home and discovered the theft he notified the police. Detective Constable Green interviewed the defendant who denied ever having been at the house. The prosecution asks you to come to the conclusion that it was the defendant who committed the offence as he was seen there at a time when he had no right to be there and he then lied to the police about it. Ask yourselves why he lied? Surely it can only be because he is guilty?

It should be possible to open a case of this sort to a jury in not much more than five minutes, but it will take some counsel three or four times as long as they will read out almost all the evidence available and make the same point a number of times; many counsel seem to believe that jurors are not very bright, however much they may make sycophantic remarks as to the jury's commonsense in their speeches. My advice at this stage is to ignore anything said about the complexities of the law and concentrate on the facts: it is much more sensible to try to apply the law when you have heard the evidence (remember, what counsel tells you is not evidence) and have an authoritative direction on the law from the Judge. Compare the opening by counsel and the evidence in the case of the burglary and theft of £10. The neighbour is called to give evidence that he saw the defendant going into the house on the day in question but, when cross-examined, admits that he might be mistaken and it could have been the day before that he had seen the defendant: end of case!

It is interesting that in Scotland, which has jury trial, the case is not opened at all. That undoubtedly saves time but I believe that a jury should be told, in outline, what the case they are about to try is about, so that the members of the jury can relate the evidence which they hear to the overall allegations. It might be a good idea if Prosecuting Counsel were not to try to explain the law at this stage but for the Judge to make a positive, authoritative statement of the law relating to the charges: he knows what it is, and why should the jury not be told it correctly at the beginning, instead of the end, of the trial? In addition, if Prosecuting Counsel were to be restricted to giving an outline without going into the detailed evidence, it would save time and simplify the whole case for the jury.

In a more complicated case, such as one of financial fraud, which may take weeks or months to try, there may be a vast number of documents, numbering often many hundreds and even thousands. This begins with the police investigation into the case, and experience has taught them that to get a conviction in a fraud case it is necessary to cross every 'T' and dot every 'I', with the result that many witnesses are called and vast collections of documents are assembled. Usually before the Magistrates' Court hearing these documents have been photocopied (it is difficult to imagine how the courts managed before photocopiers were available) and assembled in neat bundles. From then on they seem to acquire a momentum of their own. Efforts are usually made at the Crown Court by Judges and counsel to reduce the number of documents which have to go before a jury and this is often done by replacing large numbers of them, especially where they are, for example, weekly returns, by a schedule, the accuracy of which both the prosecution and defence accept. Much has been said and written about juries having the ability to deal with cases of this sort. It is not, in my opinion, so much the inherent ability of the jurors as the unnecessary length and complication which wears down jurors (and Judges) as well as the tactics sometimes adopted by the defence which are aimed at increasing the confusion: that we will examine later. Look at the large bundles of documents, examine the ones to which your attention is directed but, in making your decisions at the end of the case, you will probably find that you will be considering only a handful of them, if any.

In a typical long fraud case (many are not really fraud cases but straightforward thefts with complicated 'bookkeeping' to attempt to disguise the theft) there is usually more than one defendant and the prosecution and at least one of the principal defendants will be represented each by two counsel. As I have said, Queen's Counsel normally undertake the longer and more difficult cases but their very presence seems to create an aura which results in cases in which they are involved lasting even longer. They attempt to, or naturally, give to a case an air of gravity and importance which it may not merit: any Judge who is frank would concede that a couple of leading counsel will add anything from 25% to 50% to the length of a case. So, if you see serried ranks of barristers be ready for a long case, but you can always hope that you will be wrong as the number of barristers is not an infallible guide: the coming of summer holidays (known to the lawyers as the Long Vacation) can have an effect on the length of cases. On one occasion in front of an Old Bailey Judge, in his room, leading counsel for the defence told him that the case could last for three to six months, at which Prosecuting Counsel said that he had expected a plea of guilty and had planned on a holiday beginning the following week. The Judge, understandably, did not appear very keen on such a long trial and suggested that a plea of guilty would result in the defendant not going to prison. The defendant was told this, pleaded guilty, and was fined a very substantial sum which was well within his means.

This type of 'deal' was fairly common until it went too far, too often, and the Court of Appeal has made it clear on a number of occasions, such as in the cases of The Queen v. Turner in 1970 and The Queen v. Cain in 1976, that it must stop, although it still goes on in a rather less blatant fashion and much less frequently. It had its good side: a defendant would often plead guilty if he knew that he would not go to prison, so that much court time and public money was saved. It is a pity that a system can not be evolved whereby a defendant would know in advance the nature of his sentence on conviction, i.e. a fine, a community service order or a prison sentence with some idea of the upper and lower limits which would apply. Providing all this were to be done openly it could cause no offence. But this is a digression, save in so far as it may help you to understand why so many hopeless cases are fought.

Assuming that, at least in trials of this character, you

have a copy of the indictment and, certainly, copies of the documents, you will be ready to listen to the opening. If counsel starts talking about documents and you have not got them, do not hesitate to ask the Judge for copies as you are entitled to see them. In a case of this type counsel will deal with each type of charge and the evidence relating to samples of the charges sufficiently to show the pattern of the alleged crimes. Sometimes these long trials have only one charge, that of Conspiracy, that is to say the defendants are charged with planning to commit offences which are so numerous that it is easier to allege the planning than to prove strictly each separate offence, although the evidence you will hear will normally show the commission of a number of offences. Sometimes these trials lose any type of form and the evidence can be nebulous and vague; they are looked upon with some disfavour by the Court of Appeal and the charging of a number of specific charges is encouraged.

Whilst these cases can be a burden to juries, it must also be said that they can also be a burden to Judges, lawyers and defendants as well as to witnesses who may have to spend days in the witness-box, being questioned about incidents which often happened years before. It would be almost as tedious for me to attempt to outline the opening of one of these cases as it would be for you to listen to some of them but, remember, Prosecuting Counsel has a problem. A short opening and he is exposed to criticism that he has not put the prosecution case against the defendant at the beginning of the case, or a long opening and he is criticized for wasting time. The happy medium is achieved by experienced counsel who fully understands the case which he is opening. If the opening is long and rambling you may not be unjustified in having the suspicion that counsel has not mastered his brief. Interesting: but sometimes of much greater interest than what is said is what is not said in the opening.

Let us return to the simple case, although the following may apply equally to the longer one. Apart from the evidence of witnesses as to the actual incident or incidents from which the offence arises, it is usual to have evidence from a police officer, or officers, as to interviews with the defendant. So one hears, from Prosecuting Counsel, at the end of his summary of the evidence, something like this, 'Detective Constable Green saw the defendant who denied ever being at the house.' That is straightforward and fits in with the defendant's own version. But the police evidence may be different, so you hear Prosecuting Counsel say, 'When seen by the police the defendant admitted that he had taken the £10.' On hearing that you may wonder why the defendant is pleading not guilty, but you will learn later that he is alleging either that the policeman misunderstood what he had said or that the policeman is lying. Denial and admission are easy to understand. You might though, justly, be surprised when counsel says nothing at all about any police interview. In addition, at an interview, a defendant is usually asked by the police if he wishes to make a written statement about the allegations, again this can be a denial or an admission, but he can quite properly decline to do so, in which event Prosecuting Counsel will usually tell you that there is no written statement: if he says nothing at all about a written statement you should be interested. Almost in every case where you hear nothing about a police interview or a written statement it means that the defendant has made admissions but that he is now challenging their admissibility. This means that he is claiming that, for example, the written statement was written by a police officer and he was forced or tricked into signing it: if that is true then the statement is inadmissible. When this situation exists Defence Counsel tells Prosecuting Counsel that there will be a challenge to the admissibility of the statement so that Prosecuting Counsel will not refer to it in his opening address as, at a later stage, as we will see, the Judge has to decide whether or not the statement is admissible. If it is, you will hear its contents, otherwise you won't. If there is no mention of a statement or of an interview with the police you can be certain that the defendant has admitted his guilt but is now attempting to retract his admission. You will hear more about this later in the case.

5

Evidence and Rules: General Features

Having concluded his opening Prosecuting Counsel will start to call his witnesses to give evidence which will, it is hoped, establish the allegations made against the defendant. One of the main tasks which counsel has is to ensure that the witnesses give their own evidence, remember it is not what counsel says that is important but the evidence the witnesses give, so the first rule is that counsel may not ask leading questions. A leading question is not, as some people think, an awkward question, but one which, within itself, suggests the answer: for example, to ask, 'Did the man have black hair?' suggests that he did, whilst, 'What colour hair did the man have?' does not suggest the answer and leaves it to the witness to give an unprompted answer. In fact it often results in the witness giving an answer which was unexpected, or in the witness not being able to remember. There are exceptions to this rule such as where there is no dispute between prosecution and defence over a particular piece of evidence. In that case counsel will have discussed it between themselves beforehand or you may hear Defence Counsel say to the Judge, 'My learned friend may lead this witness' or 'Your Honour, there is no dispute about this witness's evidence', so that time is saved and the witness does not have to search his memory to recall the facts. Often the first question asked of a witness is something along these lines, 'Is your name Zandra Abigail White, are you a shop assistant and do you live at 47 Southampton Street, Liverpool?' Counsel has read those details from the head of the statement he has of that witness, which may well have been made many months before, to be met with the answer, 'No'. Does the 'No' relate to the whole question, has the wrong person come into the witness-box (that has happened), or is the 'No' an answer to the name, the occupation or the address? If nothing else it shows the dangers of asking three questions in one. It also shows the superiority of the proper method of asking one question at a time. 'What is your name?' 'What is your occupation?' 'What is your address?' All three could change in the time between the making of the statement and the coming into the witness-box to give evidence, the name by marriage, the occupation and address for obvious reasons. Another advantage of asking a witness questions to which he knows the answers without effort is that it helps him to establish confidence in giving evidence.

Counsel will then go on to ask the witness questions so as to elucidate the evidence; sometimes it is necessary for the witness to refer to exhibits in the case, for example the stolen property, or, in a fraud case, to documents. Examination-in-chief, as this is called, is one of the most difficult tasks that a barrister has to carry out. He has to contend with witnesses who are forgetful, vague, stupid and deliberately lying as well as those who have good memories, are clear, intelligent and truthful. The forgetful, vague and stupid can only be dealt with, if at all, with great patience, and in situations of that sort you will hear counsel attempting to extract the evidence by approaching the questions from different angles, showing the witness exhibits in the hope that they may refresh the witness's memory, sometimes with success, sometimes not. When you listen to this type of examination-in-chief you will know that the witness has not 'come up to proof' (to use the lawyers' terminology): he has forgotten an important piece of evidence about which Prosecuting Counsel has told you in his opening. Do not fall for the temptation of making good the missing evidence by using counsel's opening, that was not evidence and this shows the dangers of the system of detailed openings of cases. Patience may be a successful formula in dealing with the forgetful, vague and stupid but it does not help in dealing with the liar.

How do you know that he is lying? That is completely a matter of personal judgement in most cases but often when a prosecution witness does not come up to proof, even if he can not be proved to be lying on oath, there is a way of showing that he has told a different story on a previous occasion: note, a different story, not that on an earlier occasion he said something which he has now not said. The failure of a witness to say something in evidence may be due to forgetfulness or it may be due to deliberate omission and in some cases may mean that the prosecution can not prove a particular point, which is essential, and the Judge has to stop the case at the end of the prosecution's evidence (see Chapter 11). This is not a situation which can be cured by the production of the witness's earlier statement, which can not become evidence in that way. Sometimes, though, a witness may give evidence which is of great value to the defence, or damaging to the prosecution. If nothing has been previously said about that matter nothing can be done about it but if, on a previous occasion, either in a written statement or in giving evidence in the Magistrates' Court, he has said something contrary to that evidence then action can follow. That action will be initiated by Prosecuting Counsel saying something like, 'Your Honour, there is a matter of law which now arises.' The Judge will then turn to the jury and say, 'Members of the Jury, matters of law are for me to decide so would you please retire to your room while this matter is dealt with.' And out you go. The witness may be asked to leave the court so that he will not hear the argument. The defendant will remain in court as he will at all times.

What is happening in court whilst you are in your room? Prosecuting Counsel will draw the Judge's attention to a previous statement made by the witness and argue that he is now telling a story which is contrary to the one he told earlier and will apply that the witness (the prosecution's own) be treated as a 'hostile' witness: this means 'hostile', not just unfavourable. The Judge will compare the statement with what the witness has said in evidence, listen to both counsel argue for and against, and then decide whether or not to allow the prosecution to treat the witness as hostile. If he decides against the prosecution application it means that when you return to court you will hear nothing more about the matter but, if the Judge decides in the prosecution's favour, the previous statement will be put to the witness so as to discredit the evidence he has given in court: note, the prosecution discredits its own witness and asks you not to believe him. You will note that the Judge's permission, or 'leave' as the lawyers usually call it, is necessary to allow a counsel to attack his own witness whilst witnesses for the other side can always be attacked in cross-examination by being shown previous statements that they have made. Despite all this, you will still have to decide whether or not the witness told the truth in court, whatever he may have said in a statement on a previous occasion. The whole procedure is not really so mysterious: either you will hear the two versions or, if not, you will know he has said something different on another occasion although, not in the Judge's view, so much

50

different as to allow the witness to be treated as hostile. We will return to the question of what happens when you are out of court in more detail in Chapter 10.

When examination-in-chief has been concluded it is the turn of Defence Counsel, if there is more than one defendant then counsel in turn, to ask questions of the witnesses: this is described as cross-examination and has different objectives from examination-in-chief and one major variation to the rules as to questioning. The objects of cross-examination are principally twofold. First, to attempt to get a witness to agree that he was wrong in what he had said, or in part of what he had said, in his examination-in-chief, or at least to modify that evidence. Secondly, to ask him questions which will lead to additional information favourable to the defence. It is very rare for a witness to admit, under cross-examination, that he was wrong in essential matters in his examination-in-chief, although it does happen with perfectly honest witnesses. Sometimes showing a witness a written document, which the prosecution did not have, may refresh his memory so that he agrees he was mistaken regarding the date of a transaction, or reminding a witness of a further fact can lead to a change in his evidence. Modification of evidence or an apparent less sureness of his recollection is more often the case after cross-examination which, despite the 'cross', can most effectively be carried out, on most occasions, in a very quiet tone of voice without any appearance of hostility. There are, of course, exceptions to this. It can be a fascinating experience to watch a skilled advocate cross-examining. He will start by trying to establish a rapport with the witness and go through those parts of the evidence which are not in dispute, then carefully get nearer to the parts he has to challenge. One thing the advocate can not do is to prepare his questions in advance: he does not know exactly what the witness will say in examination-in-chief nor to the first question he puts to him in cross-examination. The experienced barrister will have in mind, or noted, the subjects he has to deal with, and knows his objectives, but has to make up his questions as he goes along, settling for half-favourable answers when he can see that he is not going to get a fully favourable one.

One tactic you should look out for in complicated financial frauds is the advocate-inspired muddle. A witness may have given evidence clearly and explained the documents and the accounts so that everyone believes that they understand them but, in cross-examination, Defence Counsel questions him with the documents taken out of order, refers back and forth from one to another, without any system, and, if the defence has any other documents, shows them to the witness and, when complete confusion has been achieved, says to the witness, 'Thank you, Mr Green, it is now quite clear to me.' You may wonder if you have misunderstood the whole thing: ignore cross-examination of that type, it is only designed to confuse and to cover up the fact that there is no defence. The defence hope is that either the jury will acquit due to the confusion or that the Judge will become confused and get his summing-up wrong at the end of the case and the defendant will, consequently, be able to have his conviction quashed on appeal.

However, not all cross-examination is helpful to a defendant, either because the cross-examination is not very skilful or, simply, because the longer a witness is in the witness-box the more confident he may become and the more his memory may return to him. In addition, if counsel has been unsuccessful in the soft approach and then tries to be more direct, a witness can become annoyed and blurt out remarks about the defendant which are less than helpful to the defendant. How often, when counsel has accused a witness of lying about, say, the defendant hitting someone, that the witness says, 'It's not the only time: he did it in the Red Lion the week before!' Wise counsel will refrain from cross-examining whenever possible and then only with the greatest discretion: many cases have swung against a defendant because of unwise cross-examination. There is, though, one exception to the 'rule' regarding careful cross-examination. Some cases are, on the face of them, so hopeless that counsel has no option but just to put the instructions he has from the defendant to the witnesses strongly and clearly: there is no room for the 'softly-softly' approach or any attempt to persuade a witness to vary from his original evidence. Astonishingly, this method is not always without success.

Something which might affect you subconsciously is the manner in which counsel cross-examine witnesses. This can range from the rather vapid and pathetic, 'I put it to you that you are not telling the truth', answered with 'I am', type of questioning to a hard staccato, machine-gun-like series of questions delivered with spirit. Many judges do not like this latter method and they are usually right about that but, sometimes, it is only a hard persistent cross-examination which breaks an untruthful witness. How is the jury affected by the style of cross-examination? Conviction in the voice of anyone to whom we are listening is important. If you hear a barrister saying, 'I am sorry, Mr Grey, but it is my duty to put it to you that you are not telling the truth', you may well react with the feeling that he is apologizing for having to put the question and that he does not believe that the witness is lying: in other words he is only putting the question because he has to. On the other hand a voice, with feeling, saying, 'Mr Grey, you are lying and you have been lying in that witness-box for the last two hours', (more a statement than a question), comes over with force because the speaker gives the impression that it is his own view. This, of course, offends against the rule that counsel must not express his own view: however, when counsel is acting for a defendant he is really applying his learning, experience and skill to do what a defendant himself would do if he had the learning, experience and skill, so it could be said that counsel is doing nothing more than to articulate the defendant's own feelings. Judges have been known to say that the tone of voice counsel uses does not help. I disagree, it does, but I agree with them that it should not. Do not allow it to do so, it is not the tone of voice in which the question is asked but the tone and content of the answer which is important.

We have seen that it is not open to counsel to ask his own witness leading questions in examination-in-chief; this applies equally to Prosecuting Counsel and to Defence Counsel. The rule, though, does not apply in cross-examination where leading questions may be asked. The justification for this is not far to seek. First, the objection, which applies in examination-in-chief, that leading questions suggest answers to witnesses ceases to be an objection as cross-examining counsel is usually challenging the version which the witness has already given. Secondly, it would be almost impossible for a cross-examiner to bring the other side's witness to the matters he wishes to deal with in the same way as an examiner-in-chief, because the witness has not been interviewed by his solicitors to see what he would say. It is a necessary relaxation of the rule and saves a great deal of time.

After Defence Counsel has completed his cross-examination the prosecution has another turn. This is called re-examination but it does not entitle the prosecution to introduce fresh evidence but only to ask the witness further questions on any matters which have been dealt with in cross-examination. If Prosecuting Counsel does not re-examine it means that he is satisfied that the witness has not been shaken in cross-examination and does not need to have his evidence reinforced by repetition or that he has been so destroyed by cross-examination that to attempt to salvage anything from the wreckage would be hopeless: you will decide for yourselves which, if either, of those situations exists. When Prosecuting Counsel indicates that he has completed his re-examination, if any, that is not necessarily the end of the questioning: the Judge may ask some questions. Some ask very few questions but some have asked so many that the Court of Appeal has quashed convictions, if rather rarely, because either the defendant and/or his counsel have been prevented from presenting the defence case properly. Judges need, on occasion, to ask questions as, at the end of the case, a Judge has to sum up the evidence for the jury and he will want to be clear in his own mind what the witness is saying: that is the main reason. Some do it to underline the defendant's guilt, but it will not take you long to identify that type of Judge: generally his interventions are unnecessary for that purpose but some cannot, perhaps understandably, forget their days at the Bar. Do not allow the Judge's opinions and prejudices, if any, to influence you but, on the other hand, don't say to yourself, 'I don't like that Judge or his attitude so I'll acquit.' That would be wrong and unjust: justice means fair play for both sides. There are judges who make life difficult for everyone; they ask questions continually during the witness's evidence but, remember, Judges, on some occasions, are forced into asking questions because inefficient or inexperienced counsel are not asking the right ones. This does not always help the prosecution as Judges are frequently concerned that a defendant is not having his case put strongly or clearly enough.

Leading questions have already been mentioned: another legal word you may hear used is 'hearsay', literally a witness giving in evidence something which someone else told him. This is not, with certain exceptions, permitted. The reason is easy to see. If a witness says that he saw an event then he can be questioned about it and his accuracy and truthfulness tested; but, if he says that someone else told him that an event had taken place, he can only be tested as to his accuracy and truthfulness as to his recollection of what he has been told, not as to the event itself: the person who should give evidence is the person who actually saw the incident. The first, apparent, exception is in a witness telling the court what a defendant said on a previous occasion but that can be challenged as the defendant was there and can give his own version. The second is one which usually occurs when the defendant gives evidence (although there is no reason why it should not occur with other witnesses) and wishes to explain why he committed a particular act and to do that has to say that he was told something by someone else which led him to commit the act. It is not evidence of the truth of what he was told but, if you believe him, evidence which helps to explain his state of mind at the time.

Before leaving the question of witnesses in general it might be helpful to refer to certain remarks which are made by counsel to the Judge. When a fresh witness is called, counsel may say to the Judge, 'Your Honour, page 14.' He may add 'of the depositions or statements'. You will not have these documents: counsel is referring to the statements tendered at the Magistrates' Court (Chapter 3). Of course, if counsel refers to, say, page 23 of the exhibits then these you will, or should, have. Occasionally, instead of saying 'page 14 of depositions', counsel may say 'This is the subject of a notice of additional evidence.' It often happens that between the date of the proceedings in the Magistrates' Court and the trial at the Crown Court extra evidence becomes available to the prosecution which it desires to call at the trial. In order to be allowed to do so the prosecution serves on the defence, that is on the solicitor, a copy of the statement made by the new witness, or sometimes a second statement by an existing witness. This should be done as soon as possible after the evidence comes to hand but it is often not done until the last minute. Sometimes, as a result of the way in which the defence develops its case, the prosecution has to obtain fresh evidence during the case and serve it on the defence. This is not at all unusual in long fraud cases and, as the defendant has the right to ask for time to consider last minute evidence like this, sometimes leads to adjournments of cases to enable the defence to meet the new situation. It has not been unknown for defendants to change their pleas to guilty after the additional evidence has been served on them.

6
Expert and Special Witnesses

The types of witnesses you will see and hear will vary enormously from the nervous giving evidence for the first time to the experienced, perhaps a little arrogant, police witness with every possible intermediate gradation. When assessing a witness you will ask yourself two questions. Is he honest? Is he accurate? Make full allowance for the nervous witness, the witness under strain: it is not difficult to imagine the state of mind of a girl giving evidence of having been raped. On the other hand look out for the witness who is feigning nervousness and forgetfulness. Remember also lay witnesses, by that I am excluding police and expert witnesses, themselves fall into a number of different categories: in all of them look for error, failure of recollection and honesty.

One of the most important witnesses in many cases is the victim himself, or herself, the person injured, the girl raped, the person robbed: in all these cases look very carefully at the witness, in the overwhelming number of cases he, or she, will be telling the truth but there can be cases where the witness has reason to lie. The 'injured' person in fact started the fight and the defendant was, as he maintains, only defending himself. The 'raped' girl had been agreeable to sexual intercourse but when she got home in a mess told her mother that she had been raped. The person 'robbed' may have had money taken from him but may have alleged force, or the use of a weapon, to justify his own reaction. Also, always try to take a careful look at the evidence of friends and relatives in these cases. This does not mean to say that they are always, or normally, lying, but it does happen and very close scrutiny is necessary. Perhaps more important, and frequent, is that the truthful friend or relative may quite subconsciously slant his version of what happened in favour of his friend or relative: this is, of course, equally true of the friend or relative of the defendant.

Other lay witnesses may be formal, for example the meter reader from the Gas Board to tell you how much money there should have been in the meter: you will not often hear from witnesses of this kind as their evidence is usually agreed and read to you. You will recall that all the prosecution evidence is served on the defendant by way of written statements and the procedure nowadays is that if the defendant does not dispute a witness's evidence then he will not ask for his attendance and the statement will be read to you: it is evidence in just the same way as if the witness had gone into the witness-box and given it on oath.

Of greatest importance to you is the independent witness, the person who happened to be passing when the incident occurred, who has no connection with either the victim or the defendant and no discernible reason to lie. But consider age, alertness, the length of time able to observe the incident and the position from which he was observing. When there are many witnesses to an incident do not expect them all to see the same things: if they all said the same you would, quite justifiably, become suspicious.

Then there are the experts. Witnesses who have not seen

any of the incidents in the case but who are able to assist in various ways. The first is the engineer, although we do not see very much of him in criminal trials (more in civil actions), save in cases such as causing death by reckless driving then evidence as to the condition of motor vehicles may be given. Sometimes both sides call experts and on occasion they disagree: then you have to decide whose opinion you accept. A second expert is the accountant who, surprisingly enough, you see less of in fraud cases than you would expect. The police rarely have the assistance of accountants and rely upon the work done by police officers in the investigation. Many of them become very experienced and highly skilled at this type of work. The accountant is more often called by the defence but remember he is concerned principally with accounting procedures and attitudes; for example, an accountant in one case said that a company is not insolvent if it can borrow money: that is technically correct but in the context of a criminal trial it was arrant nonsense.

Perhaps the biggest group of expert witnesses is made up of doctors, general practitioners, casualty officers, surgeons, X-ray experts, pathologists and psychiatrists and, in some cases, you will hear evidence from more than one doctor. You will have medical evidence in cases of wounding, rape, child cruelty and, of course, murder and manslaughter. Often there will be no dispute about the evidence and it will be read to you but frequently whilst the evidence the doctor has given in his statement is not disputed the defence may wish to pose additional questions. The doctor will be called in sexual cases, to state that the girl was, or was not, a virgin before the alleged rape and to give evidence of any signs of violence: obviously in a case of rape you will be looking for evidence of bruising, cuts and abrasions although, of course, rape can take place without violence; fear is enough, so is fraud.

Jury Service

A music teacher was convicted of rape because he persuaded a female pupil to have intercourse with him as he told her, and she believed, that it would improve her voice! In cases of violence the doctor may be called to prove that the skin was broken, a technical requirement in cases of wounding, or that the extent of the injuries was such that they could be said to be serious, necessary to establish that a person has inflicted grievous bodily harm, or to explain that the injury was consistent with the use of a certain type of weapon and inconsistent, perhaps, with the defendant's version that the victim slipped and fell hitting his head on a stone! In cases alleging child cruelty where the victim is so young, often a baby, that he can not give evidence and the defendants are the parents, or one of them, medical evidence, including X-räys and their interpretation, is vital, not only as to the extent and nature of the injuries but also as to their probable causation and their being inconsistent with normal parental control.

One difficulty over medical evidence is that when a casualty is brought into a hospital the doctor is concerned with saving the life of the patient, or making good his injuries, not with thinking that in many months time he may have to give evidence about the injuries. Notes are usually made of treatment but they do not necessarily recall to the doctor's mind the injuries and their possible causation. Doctors, generally, have an in-built hesitation about giving evidence; as one put it, 'Medicine is an inexact science.' There can be various causes for a condition and different medical experts may give quite different diagnoses but you are unlikely to come up against a case where the doctors disagree with one another very profoundly, although this does occur.

One medical specialist who deserves particular mention is the psychiatrist. Psychiatry is still very much an unknown field; any psychiatrist will admit this, despite the great steps which have been taken in the last century towards understanding human behaviour. One major problem the psychiatrist has to face is that he has to rely on the word of his patient to a great extent: a doctor can see a broken leg but when a patient says that he has black-outs, subject to his medical history and sometimes information from other people, which is likely to be confirmatory (how one is able to say that a patient has never had a black-out is a mystery), the psychiatrist has to rely on his experience. Even this is not always enough and a psychiatrist, properly, produces a diagnosis which is largely based on the patient's word. Normally when a person goes to a doctor he wishes to have a genuine condition treated, but a defendant may attempt to simulate an illness to attempt to escape or reduce his responsibility for some act. The psychiatrists come into court more often after conviction or a plea of guilty, but are also called when the question of diminished responsibility arises when a defendant admits killing someone but maintains that because of his mental condition it was manslaughter, not murder, as in the notorious Yorkshire Ripper case. Where there is a psychiatric issue you can expect that both sides will call experts, sometimes more than one each and, as I have said, because psychiatry is still to some extent an experimental field, (comparatively little is yet known about the brain), it is not surprising that the psychiatrists often differ. Experienced defence solicitors, particularly where there is a plea of guilty, known which psychiatrist in their area is the best to whom to refer a defendant to get the psychiatric report most favourable to that defendant.

The next group of experts cover such a wide variety of disciplines and, from the number of times many of them give evidence, can almost be described as professional witnesses, the forensic scientists. The Home Office has Forensic Science Laboratories throughout the country which give assistance to the police and to others. Their standards are high and they preserve a completely neutral attitude towards their work. Naturally, one hears them in court mainly giving evidence of scientific investigation which is damaging to a defendant; if it is not damaging to him it is generally irrelevant to the case: often negative results from forensic scientific examination results in persons not being brought to court at all, either because it does not incriminate them or may positively indicate innocence. Evidence from officers of the Forensic Science Laboratories can cover almost any subject as they have experts in most disciplines, but the most common to be heard are those dealing with blood specimens, glass fragments, paint, handwriting (see Chapter 8) and drugs.

Examination of blood samples arises in cases of wounding and in sexual cases. Classification of blood, providing the sample available is large enough, can nowadays be very precise but at the end of the day all it can establish is that the specimen is not from the defendant or that it could be from the defendant, never, positively, that it is. Even if the particular blood category of the specimen is only common to 2% of the population it does not prove that it is the defendant's as there would still be another million people in the same category in the United Kingdom. But, of course, this will not be the only evidence to connect the defendant with the crime. Typical of wounding cases is the finding of blood on the defendant's clothing which is of the same blood group as the wounded person and then you will hear evidence of them having been fighting: the problem the defendant has to face is explaining how the blood got on to his clothing. In sexual cases you may hear of specimens of spermatozoa being found on the clothing of the victim or on swabs taken from her, and this can be classified in the same way as blood specimens but, naturally, with the same restrictions. Less common, but not unknown, is the classification of a person's blood group by examination of a specimen of spittle. One of the best known instances of blood sampling is that taken in cases of driving under the influence of alcohol. These tests differ from the ones we have just mentioned as it is irrelevant to which blood group the blood belongs; the concern is purely the amount of alcohol in the blood (something which can also be determined by examination of a urine sample). Nowadays all the 'breathalyser' cases (known as such as a preliminary positive specimen of breath is normally obtained before a demand for a blood or urine sample can be made) are dealt with in the Magistrates' Courts but you may hear evidence of the level of alcohol in a person's blood in cases of causing death by reckless driving: however, even this evidence will usually now be read to you.

Scientific examination of glass fragments usually figures in two sets of circumstances. First, for example, when a window has been broken in the course of a burglary and glass fragments are found in the soles of the defendant's shoes, the scientist will be able to tell you that the window glass and the fragments have the same refractive index to which, say, 15% of all such glass belongs: again the glass fragments could have come from the broken window, not that they did. Glass fragments often figure in motor vehicle cases to attempt to show that glass at the scene of an accident came from the headlights of the suspected vehicle. Paint samples may well feature in the same investigation and the scientists are able to give evidence of the paint layers of the control sample and the suspect sample in such detail that there can be no doubt that they have the same common origin.

Another expert whom you may encounter who is not a witness is the interpreter. It is not infrequent that a defendant or a witness does not have sufficient command of English, or may speak none at all, to enable him to do justice to what he wishes to say or, if a defendant, to understand what is going on, so the services of an interpreter are obtained. There does not appear to be any regular system of obtaining interpreters but many courts, and the police, have lists of interpreters. The police will often need the assistance of interpreters in the investigation of crime and sometimes such an interpreter has to be called as a prosecution witness. Interpreters are needed much less often for the major European languages than for Chinese, Farsi, Somali or some Arabic dialect. What is unacceptable is that there is no system of ensuring that the interpreter is qualified to carry out his duties: this could be cured but no one in the system appears to be responsible for this service. Most West European court systems are very strict on this question and would not accept the makeshift way in which it is run in our courts.

Two major difficulties arise in cases with interpreters. First, lawyers put great weight on particular words, as you will discover when you hear their speeches, and in translation a misleading meaning of a word or sentence may be conveyed which can be of importance, so treat translated evidence with caution, especially where it relates to a person's feelings or reasons for taking certain steps. Secondly, in many cases a witness, or defendant, who speaks no English, is very much at sea in the whole surroundings and well-meaning interpreters, who sometimes know the witness or defendant, start to tell you what they think the witness wishes to say rather than what he is, in fact, saying. It is not unknown for a question to be posed, for it to be translated to the witness, who then delivers a short speech in, say, Arabic, and for the interpreter to translate it as 'No'! It may be an accurate summary of the answer and most helpful but it is not an interpretation. If this sort of thing happens it might not be inappropriate for you to ask the Judge if a competent interpreter could be provided. If you are dissatisfied by the standard of interpretation and no one is prepared to do anything about it the wisest thing might be to take no decision adverse to the defendant based on that evidence. In any event, you might feel that in any case with translated evidence it is dangerous to act on one answer. One other type of interpreter you may encounter is one where a witness is deaf and dumb: here there is no problem in obtaining experienced professionals and they are of a very high standard.

You might be unfortunate enough to have a witness who is mentally handicapped: this sometimes happens in cases where a nurse in a mental hospital is alleged to have assaulted a patient. Efforts are made to try to avoid the necessity of calling such witnesses but, if it is necessary, you must exercise the greatest care in acting on their evidence. You will obviously make full allowance for their condition but should weigh very carefully their evidence before you convict.

A witness you are much more likely to encounter is the child witness. Children can be extremely good witnesses, clear and without guile, but there are children who lie, some who cannot distinguish fact from fiction and the law is very careful over them, particularly where they are the alleged victims of sexual assaults. The first question which may arise in court concerns the age of the child as, before a child can give sworn evidence, the Judge has to be satisfied that the child understands the meaning of telling the truth. The questioning might go like this:

'Do you know what it means to tell the truth?'
'Yes.'
'Do you know that if you promise to tell the truth you have to?'
'Yes.'

There are many variations on this type of questioning: Judges ask the children their ages, schools and other questions to try to establish their general intelligence. Many also ask about their belief in God: whether they go to church or Sunday school and it is not uncommon for a judge not to allow a child to take the oath because of a lack of religious belief. This lack of religious belief in the child witness is hardly surprising in present-day Britain but it can result in a highly intelligent child not being sworn whilst a relatively stupid one, who says that he believes in God, is sworn. This would not matter if there was any provision for a child to affirm in the same way as an adult. This would be easy to reform: a Judge should only be expected to be satisfied that the child is of an age and intelligence to understand the need to tell the truth and then the child could be allowed to be sworn or to make an affirmation. In any even it is rare for children much under ten years of age to be sworn. The importance of swearing a child is that if the child is not sworn then his evidence has to be corroborated by some other independent evidence. If there is nothing else against a defendant than the unsworn evidence of a child then the Judge will have to stop the case at the end of the prosecution evidence. In sexual cases, even when the child has been sworn, the Judge will tell you that you must look for corroboration, but that it is open to you to convict without it but you must be very careful. One thing you can be sure of, no counsel whether prosecuting or defending, is particularly fond of examining or cross-examining children in sexual cases. You may notice the reluctance of children in many sexual cases to describe what happened. This is sometimes due to difficulty over vocabulary, they know the children's names for the sexual organs but are frightened or too embarrassed to use them. They may also be reluctant, especially in family sexual cases, perhaps because of pressure before the trial, but they can also give the same impression when they have lied on a previous occasion and now do not wish to repeat the lies. As always it will be for you to decide, as jurors, where the truth lies.

7

Police and Similar Witnesses

In virtually every case which is heard in the Crown Court, that is before a jury, you will hear evidence from police officers and/or from others who are employed in investigating duties, such as Officers of Customs and Excise. Let us deal with police witnesses first and return, later, to the other categories of professional investigators.

The United Kingdom, unlike most countries, does not have a unified police force, but a number of independent forces varying in size and character according to the areas in which they operate. The largest of these forces is the Metropolitan Police, responsible for Greater London, which is directly answerable to the Home Secretary: other forces have to report to police committees locally set up but in reality all are under a considerable degree of government control through financial grants from central government and the requirement, controlled by HM Inspectors of Constabulary, that certain standards are maintained. Like so many features in modern British society outward appearances belie reality. Standards, and methods, do vary a little from force to force but generally they are very high: criticism can often be levelled at individual officers who do not come up to the high standards expected of them and we have seen, over the years, how the police force deals with its own offenders.

Whilst, as members of the general public, we can take satisfaction in those standards, although being concerned about failures, the juror is concerned not with general standards but, where police evidence is challenged, whether or not that particular officer, or those officers, have lived up to those standards. The juror is concerned with a specific situation, not with generalities. It would be well to remember that the vast majority of persons charged with criminal offences plead guilty and do not challenge the police at all and that those who do plead not guilty more often than not still do not challenge the police or, if they do, it is as likely to be to their recollections as to their honesty. In the end it is a small minority who accuse police officers of lying. This tends, on the one hand, to support the thesis that police evidence is nearly always truthful but, on the other hand, the cynic might reply that when the accusation is made it is all the more likely to be true. In order to decide whether or not a police officer is lying, it would be best for you as a juror to put aside any preconceived notions and decide purely on the merits of what you hear in the case. Look at, listen to the police officers and the defendant and any other evidence which supports one side or the other, then make up your own mind.

There are two basically different situations in which a police officer may become involved in giving evidence: first, where a crime is reported to the police and the officer sent to investigate; secondly, where the officer is himself involved in the incident, such as where the defendant is alleged to have assaulted the officer. It is usually in the second category that allegations of lying are made against police officers and, you will appreciate, that there can be reasons for police officers to lie in such cases: the police can be at fault and blame the defendant. When allegations are made of police lying in the first category, which do occur, you might ask yourself 'Why should the police lie?'

The police witnesses you will see and hear will vary enormously as to age, experience and rank and also according to their roles in the police force. There are great differences between the traffic policeman, the dog-handler, the ordinary uniformed officer on the beat and the detective. This arises inevitably from the different nature of their tasks and, perhaps, also from their own personal characteristics which have led them into the various branches. The nature of their employment is also reflected in their familiarity with giving evidence in the Crown Court: it is not uncommon to find a uniformed Inspector to be giving evidence in the Crown Court for the second or third time only, whilst a Detective Constable may already have done so on a dozen or more occasions. Police officers employed on traffic duties will be called as witnesses in cases involving motor vehicles, but it is not uncommon for such cases to turn into ones of violence, where it is alleged that the driver has attacked a police officer, so the police officer on traffic duties may turn up to give evidence on two different aspects of such a case: there is no hard and fast division, traffic officers are police officers. Cases of violence will more often than not be dealt with by uniformed officers as will most cases of petty dishonesty, whilst the Criminal Investigation Department will deal with the more serious cases of dishonesty, fraud and, of course, such matters as conspiracy and murder. Allegations of offences relating to vice, such as living off immoral earnings, or dealing in drugs will usually be investigated by officers from special vice and drugs squads. None of these categories is exclusive: on one occasion I heard of an Assistant Chief Constable being involved in arresting a man trying to drive off a car which did not belong to him whilst, at the other extreme, a major corruption and fraud enquiry, which lasted for several years and took up several months of court-time, started because of suspicions a junior detective had of the activities of a local government employee, who turned out to be completely innocent, but this led to the main investigation. There is perhaps only one thing that all policemen, good or bad, honest or dishonest, have in common: they all carry notebooks.

During the course of a year a police officer, particularly a busy detective, may well deal with many dozens of incidents and have conversations with many people; thus he may have spoken to the defendant in the trial you are hearing six or more months previously and by the time of the trial would find it almost impossible to recollect what had been said in that conversation. As a result the practice has grown up over the years, blessed by the courts, of allowing witnesses, not only police officers, to refresh their memories by referring to notes which they have made contemporaneously. 'Contemporaneously' is a word which has been interpreted by the courts rather differently from that of the compiler of a dictionary: two weeks after the event has been held to be contemporaneous but, obviously, the nearer to the time of the incident that the note was made the greater the reliance that can be placed on it. Watch closely what happens when the police officer goes into the witness-box. First, like everyone else, he takes the oath, sometimes a little militarily, as if by doing it in that fashion it will carry greater weight with a jury, then he gives his name, rank and other details and, then, notice that he will, almost certainly, have a notebook in his hand. However, a witness is not allowed to make use of a note without the leave of the Judge, so you will hear Prosecuting Counsel say something like this:

'Officer, you have a notebook in your hand. Do you wish to

make use of it to refresh your memory as to the incidents in this case and the conversations you had with the defendant?'
'Yes, sir,' comes the answer.
'When did you make the notes up?'
'Shortly after each conversation.'
'Did you make the notes up at the earliest possible opportunity?'
'Yes, sir.'
Counsel will then address the Judge. 'May the officer use his notebook, Your Honour?'

The object of these questions is to establish that the officer needs the notes that he made up at the first possible opportunity. These are formal questions and do not establish the truth of what is in the note. If the officer is a liar then it does not matter when he made up the note but, if he is a truthful witness, even if mistaken, then the errors are likely to be less the earlier the note has been written. You may also hear another question from Prosecuting Counsel, 'Did you make up the note on your own?' Answer, 'No, sir. I made it up with Detective Constable Black.' This has been held to be perfectly proper by the Court of Appeal, that is to say where two officers have been present at an interview that they should get together to try to remember accurately what was said: two heads being better than one. This is not necessarily true: if the stronger of the two is mistaken in his recollection then the other may follow his lead and the opportunity to check the accuracy of their recollections has been lost. It is surprising, when two officers have not made their notes up together, how common it is that there are substantial differences, even where both are completely honest and doing their best to recollect what had been said. This situation occurs when the defendant does not deny what the police say was said at the interview but alleges that something additional was said: neither policeman has it in his notebook but one will remember that something was said whilst the other, genuinely, has no recollection of it.

One of the difficulties about this whole subject is that much passes between police officers and defendants which is, on any basis, irrelevant: when the police spend hours with a defendant this is inevitable. But the police, understandably, make up their notes on what to them, at that time, seems relevant to their enquiry. Later other matters which they did not realize were important become so, especially as they cannot know what may be important to the defence. So there are advantages and disadvantages in the combined note-taking method. The only absolutely safe way is for everything which passes between the investigating officers and the defendant either to be taken down in shorthand or recorded on tape: even this would lead to allegations of tampering with the shorthand record or manipulating the tape. In any event, one is reluctant to recommend any course which would lengthen trials because anyone who believes that tape recording would settle the matter does not know defendants who contest almost any allegations, particularly when they have no real defence.

In the normal course of events an officer will make up his notebook (a phrase which they so often use and which has an unfortunate sound about it) and from that note he will prepare his statement of evidence for the committal proceedings in the Magistrates' Court: the result being that his notebook, his statement and the evidence he gives in the Crown Court will be almost word for word the same and is the reason why many Prosecuting Counsel, once having the officer sworn, just let him read from his notebook, that is after the Judge has given his leave. When the officer has made his notebook up with another officer it means that you will hear identical evidence twice but, in fact, where there is no dispute you will not hear the second officer give evidence or, if you do, only so that he can be cross-examined. It is not infrequent when two officers collaborate to make up a note that it is only written in the one officer's notebook and the second officer initials the note and then uses it to refresh his memory.

One other form of note, relied upon by police officers on traffic duties, is a small special accident report notebook which can be used to record details of a particular traffic accident. It has room and special provision for sketches, details of damage to the various vehicles and answers given by the drivers to questions put to them. These notebooks are more often used in the Magistrates' Courts, where all traffic cases are dealt with, save causing death by reckless driving which is heard in the Crown Court.

It was quite understandable that in the very early days of the police force, officers made notes to remind themselves of incidents: over the years the system has become formalized, indeed almost institutionalized, so that what started off as an aid to the police officer has now become a principal weapon, in the hands of Defence Counsel, to attack police officers. In some police forces, I do not know if in all, officers are expected to put in their notebooks the times they go on and off duty, times of meal breaks and everything else which occurs, and the notebook has to be available for inspection, and is inspected, by the officer's superiors. Others, particularly detectives, use the book as it was originally intended, to put in notes which the officer himself needs to refresh his memory. One of the undesirable effects of the system of examination of the notebook by an officer's superiors is the obsession of some officers to keep it neat and tidy and, as a result, sometimes the notebooks are made up later from rough notes the officer made up at the time of the incident. If you see the officer's notebook – and, if he is challenged on it by Defence Counsel who examines it and then questions him on it, you have the right to see it, otherwise you cannot judge whether the points Defence Counsel is making are good or bad – have a close look to see how tidily it is kept: if very tidy then the chances are that the officer has not told the truth that the notebook was made up at the first possible opportunity. Do not forget, though, that if there are alterations in the notebook the officer will be attacked, or at least criticized, for the amendments: in the hands of Defence Counsel he cannot win!

The Judge may be reluctant to let you see the officer's notebook; this may be for one of two reasons: one, that the defence point is so bad and the answers so good that it will purely waste your time (this is a rather unlikely reason as, in those circumstances most Judges would rather you see it) or, two, that there is something in the notebook which you must not see because it incriminates the defendant, perhaps in some other crime. In Chapter 4 I mentioned that the defendant may have pleaded guilty to some other charge or charges and the officer's notebook may have some reference to those affairs of which you are not supposed to be aware. If you are not allowed to see the notebook after you have specifically asked to see it then you can be certain that there is material in it which will act to the detriment of the defendant. Why though does the police officer's notebook play such a large part in the criminal trial?

It is not unfair that Defence Counsel should wish to compare an officer's evidence in the trial with what he recorded in his notebook, say, some six months earlier. Why though, you will ask, should he try as the officer will only be reading out of his notebook? Strictly speaking that is correct, but experience has shown that there are occasions when discrepancies between notebooks, statements and evidence occur. Nearly all these discrepancies are totally innocent and irrelevent, a few are not and even some of the innocent errors can be made, by clever Defence Counsel, to look suspicious. The end result of the discrepancies may not affect the evidence but the object of cross-examination of this type is to shake the jury's faith in the officer's integrity or accuracy, or both, so that the jury finds it cannot accept his evidence on matters where there are no discrepancies. This line of cross-examination usually occurs when Defence Counsel has no other worthwhile line of cross-examination and begins by asking the officer, 'May I see your notebook, officer?' Counsel has the right to see it if the officer has used it: if he read up the note outside court immediately before coming in to give his evidence counsel will not have the right to see it, although he can always ask the officer if he is prepared to produce it: if the officer refuses then comment will, undoubtedly, be made about that refusal in Defence Counsel's closing speech. There is no restriction on a police officer, or any other witness, looking at his notebook which he will have with him or at the statement he made for the Magistrates' Court proceedings, a copy of which will be in the possession of the Prosecution Solicitor, before he comes into court providing that he asks to see it: somehow it is thought wrong for him to see it if he does not specifically ask to see it, in other words, it is wrong for the prosecution to offer it to him! This is got around by the police officer in the case, or the prosecuting solicitor or his clerk, telling witnesses that they can ask to see their statements if they want to! Whereupon they make the request.

The arguments *pro* and *con* the notebook are considerable. On the one hand it would be wrong for an officer to have to rely on his unaided memory after a long period whilst, on the other hand, the trial may turn into trial by notebook. Generally speaking, you will find that police officers make reasonably accurate and, above all, truthful notes but a note made up even five minutes after a conversation cannot be completely reliable.

Try it yourself (perhaps not in the jury room): conduct a short conversation, say for two minutes, and record it on a cassette recorder. Try then to write down what had been said and then compare it with the recording. This will demonstrate how difficult it is. Remember, though, that many police officers, particularly detectives, have experience at this task which can help them to make their notes more accurate. Some officers will maintain that their notes are word perfect: this is almost impossible unless the words are taken down at the time they are spoken. Good, honest police officers will say straightaway, 'I did my best and I got the gist of it but I don't claim to be word perfect.'

Many hours, even days, can be taken up in a trial with the evidence of police officers, their notebooks and their written statements all being compared. Look to see if there are any differences of substance: do not get excited when the times differ by five minutes, unless time is the essential point. The vast majority of cross-examinations of this kind are carried out by Defence Counsel on 'fishing' expeditions, where there is no real substance to the defence, in the hope that something will turn up. Occasionally, very occasionally, something does turn up but, usually, if there is anything to the point the defence will already have known about it. If a point of substance does turn up, act on it: if not, then you have a good idea that his line of cross-examination is due to a bankrupt defence. Bluntly, pure fishing exercises of this type are an abuse of the system and Judges should step in more often to prevent them. In any event the jury can deal with them in an appropriate way in arriving at its verdict.

The police are not the only 'professional' witnesses who you may hear. In addition you may hear evidence from officers of Customs and Excise, particularly in drug cases, Post Office investigators and others, including store detectives in shop-lifting cases. Customs and Excise officers work very closely with the police on their cases and the only difference between them is that they are more familiar with the technicalities of the law on, for example, drugs than the police but usually less familiar with giving evidence, but they certainly impress as being efficient and reliable. Post Office investigators are usually to be found in cases involving thefts by sub-postmasters and postmistresses and with postmen who steal from the mails. They have a very sensible system when they interview suspects of writing down all the questions and answers and asking the suspect to read them and sign them, each one of them, if he or she agrees that they are correct. You might think that would end any dispute over what had been said, but you would be wrong: the defendant will say that he or she was upset and that he or she did not know what he or she was saying or signing. It would not be a bad idea, though, if this system was more generally followed. It must be admitted however that there is no fool- (or defendant-) proof system to avoid later disputes.

A witness who causes many advocates disquiet is the store detective, for reasons which may or may not be valid. There is a feeling that they have a duty to catch a quota of people and that, if they catch no one, they might lose their posts and that, as a result, they arrest innocent people. This may sometimes happen; we will never be certain, although there have been occasions when counsel have felt some disquiet and so, apparently, have juries. Perhaps the disquiet is caused, in part, by the fact that all the other investigators are employed by the police and government departments with certain standards in force as to conduct and training, whilst store detectives may vary greatly as to their competence and the standards expected by their employers. Usually in shop-lifting cases the dispute is over whether the defendant said something incriminating to the

81

store detective and whether or not the defendant genuinely forgot to pay for the item or items.

You may wonder why a case involving a tin of sardines, value 25 pence, or a tin of salmon, value £1.25 (it is noticeable, in fact, that people usually forget to pay for the more expensive items) is being tried in the Crown Court and not in the Magistrates' Court. This is because a charge of theft is only triable in the Crown Court unless the defendant agrees to it being tried in the Magistrates' Court: it is the nature of the charge, dishonesty, and not the value of the goods which dictates the court of trial. Fortunately most of these small cases are dealt with in the Magistrates' Courts otherwise the Crown Courts would be in great difficulty. In the Magistrates' Courts trials of shop-lifting cases are much shorter than in the Crown Court, partly perhaps because the simpler cases are tried there but, more importantly, because of the absence of a Judge, jury, counsel and all the procedural features of a Crown Court trial. Many people, either if they can afford it or are legally aided without having to contribute, decide, often on legal advice, to be tried in the Crown Court because they feel that they have a better chance of a fair trial there than in the Magistrates' Court or, perhaps, that they have a better chance to pull the wool over the eyes of a 'raw' jury than over the eyes of experienced magistrates. In any event, as a juror, you have to try the case in front of you, not to worry why it is there.

8

Identification

In the vast majority of cases there is no dispute as to identity. The defendant is not denying that he was the cashier at the shop but that he did not take the money or, in an assault case, he is not denying that he struck a blow but that he did it in self-defence. So that in those cases you are concerned not with identity but with the nature of the act. There are, though, cases where the defendant says quite simply, 'It wasn't me' or 'I was somewhere else.' We will examine the matter in Chapter 9 from the defendant's point of view, where he raises 'alibi' as a defence; but, first, we will examine the ways in which the prosecution will try to prove it was the defendant and that he was at the scene of the crime. When you come to make your decision, you will naturally weigh up the prosecution's 'proof' of identity and the defendant's 'alibi' evidence against each other.

Questions of identification are ones which worry the public and the courts because there have been cases over the years, in many countries, where people have been wrongly convicted on lying, or mistaken, identification evidence: there is little that can be done about lying evidence other than in any other case of lying witnesses, but special efforts are made to try and ensure that mistaken evidence of identity is detected or excluded and we will have a look at this when we deal with the various methods of identifying defendants. A person's identity may be established by the evidence of a witness who saw the offence committed or it may be by other evidence, such as fingerprints, connecting the defendant with the offence. Let us look at the situation where a witness purports to identify the defendant as the person who committed the offence.

This might be done by the witness going up to a police officer immediately after the offence has been committed and indicating the defendant to that officer or it may be many weeks later that he again sees the defendant and then reports that fact to the police. You, of course, have at the end to decide whether or not the identification is accurate. How do you go about? The first question to ask yourself is, 'How well, if at all, did the witness know the defendant before the incident?' In many cases it is not really identification but recognition that you are dealing with. The witness knows the defendant by name and address, or, whilst he may not know these details, has seen the defendant several times a week in the same public house. If the witness is being honest this type of case should cause you no trouble. The second group of questions, if it is a case of identification, not recognition, is, 'What was the nature of the observation?', 'How long did he see the suspect?' 'How far away was he?', 'What was the light like?', 'Was the situation a calm one or a confused one?' A third question you might like to ask yourself is. 'Is there anything peculiar about the appearance of the defendant which aids identification?' Height, very tall or very short, obese, does he limp, long or short hair, has he a beard and other such matters, remembering that it is often the overall impression of a person which we recall rather than any specific feature. Needless to say the Judge, in his summing-up, will give you a long and careful warning on this subject. Another feature which might help you is if there is identification by more than one witness, providing you can be satisfied that the identifications are independent of each other. If, for example, a husband and wife identify the same person it might be that one is convinced, quite innocently, by the other that the defendant is the person who committed the offence.

Those then are the dangers involved in identification evidence: what then about the mechanics of the process? It is necessary to examine how the prosecution obtains witnesses who are able to identify a defendant. The first I have mentioned, where a witness reports to the police the identity of the defendant and will be able to give evidence quite simply of the facts and the culprit in his testimony: I am not going to go into the technicalities of the law in relation to this as they will be dealt with by the Judge and, if you need to know any of them, he will tell you, but in situations of this type you are unlikely to be worried by them.

The second is where the police have no name and no suspect, purely a description of a white man, about 5 ft 9 in in height, heavily built, long hair, about twenty-five years of age. In this case they will show photographs, necessarily of persons who have been previously convicted, as they will have no others, to the witness so that he can try to pick out the offender. There are strict rules laid down for this procedure and, if possible, that is if the defendant agrees, an identification parade should be held to give the witness the opportunity of trying to identify the defendant even though he has made a photographic identification. It is surprising how often a photograph may look like the offender but the subject of the photograph, in the flesh, may not. This also avoids the necessity of the witness saying that he picked out the defendant from a photograph which would, in effect, reveal that the defendant has a criminal record.

The third is where the police already have a suspect in custody: this is where the normal identification parade arises. The rules for holding such parades are strict and provide, amongst other things, that the suspect can have his solicitor present and that the other members of the parade must be similar in appearance to the suspect: there are a large number of technical requirements before the parade can be said to have been properly conducted and if any one of them has been infringed, Defence Counsel will soon let you know! A list of the names and addresses of the other persons who were on the identity parade is kept and you may well see the document with the details on it: unfortunately no 'group' photograph is taken which would enable you to see how homogeneous the group was. Of course, the defendant and his solicitor can object to the composition of the group at the identification parade, but it is not an occasion on which objection is gladly heard as one must realize the difficulties the police have in getting sufficient members of the public to attend who bear any resemblance to some defendants. It may be that in the end most of these precautions serve little or no purpose, but they may, and for that reason the police are very careful in conducting these parades. Remember attention is concentrated on the occasions when an identification is made not so much on the occasions when no identification is made by a witness.

It must not be forgotten that a suspect has the right to decline to go on an identification parade, his excuse for refusing, sometimes, is that he does not trust the police who will 'rig' the whole affair. It would be impossible to say that no police officer has ever acted irregularly in the conduct of such a parade but the precautions are considerable and the reason, in 99% of the cases, why a defendant declines to go on a parade is that he is afraid that he will be, correctly, identified as the culprit: the most obvious reason is usually the correct one. If he does not go on an identification parade then the police may bring witnesses, individually, to see the defendant in a cell or police interview room. If they point out the defendant it is evidence of identification but you may think not as satisfactory as at a parade. Even an honest witness who is not quite sure may have his feelings reinforced by saying to himself, 'It must be him, otherwise he would not be in the police station.' The same objection applies when the first time a witness identifies a defendant is in the Crown Court: the defendant is seated between two prison officers in the dock! The courts have never been too fond of this type of identification and nowadays it is normally prohibited both in the Crown Court and at the committal proceedings in the Magistrates' Court. One of the most frustrating scenes in a trial is a patently honest, good witness not being allowed to tell the jury that the man he is talking about is the defendant because, perhaps, the defendant has declined to attend an identification parade and the police were not able to arrange a confrontation. Experienced Prosecuting Counsel though can go a long way.

'Can you describe the man you saw?'
'Yes.'
'How tall was he?'
'About 5 feet 9 inches.'
'It is difficult to give exact height. Do you see anyone in this court about the height of the man you saw?'
A quick, intelligent witness then points out the defendant. If he is not so quick then questioning goes on.
'What sort of build was he?'

The witness looks at the defendant, 'Stocky.'
And so on until counsel then says, 'Would you know that person again if you saw him?'
'Yes.'
'Just answer my next question "Yes" or "No." Do you see that person in court?'

One of two things then happens, Either the witness gets in with an answer 'Yes' or Defence Counsel is on his feet objecting. In any event you can draw your own conclusions: it was the defendant about whom the witness was speaking. Remember, though, he could be lying or mistaken. Lying witnesses are not as likely as mistaken ones in this particular. Lying witnesses usually have a motive and in those cases they will know the defendant so that identification in the sense in which we have been examining it does not apply. Mistaken witnesses can be very impressive and so convinced of their own accuracy that they may convince you. Whatever the method of personal identification listen carefully to the Judge's summing-up at the end of the case on the approach you should take to this evidence.

A defendant may be associated with an offence by evidence of a blood specimen or glass fragments in his shoes (as we saw in Chapter 6) or by identification of his handwriting or fingerprints. Handwriting examination is a very distinct speciality and arises in, for example, cases where signatures have been forged or where anonymous letters have been written. Whilst a forgery may deceive an untutored eye and even to an expert, at first sight, appear genuine, once a proper examination has been carried out, it will be exposed for what it is. It would not be appropriate to go into detail, but the handwriting expert will have enlarged photographs of the genuine signatures or writing and of the suspect ones and will be able to say, and explain, that the suspect ones are forgeries. He will also be able to say when signatures are genuine but he will be reluctant to go as far as to say that a forged signature was definitely written by the defendant, although it has strong similarities with the defendant's writing. In other words, his evidence is usually, like that of blood, to exclude any particular person rather than to provide a positive identification.

The most important method of positively identifying a defendant as having been at the scene of an incident is by means of fingerprints. The officer who you will first hear dealing with this question will usually be a Scenes of Crimes Officer: he will have collected all the physical evidence at the scene, for example, a broken padlock, a glove that has been left behind, and he will take fingerprints from the scene. With the spread of education and general knowledge, let alone the criminal novel and the television series, it is almost impossible to believe that the police still find fingerprints at the scenes of crimes, apart, of course, from those which you would expect to be there such as those of the owner of the property.

Fingerprints are only of use to the police when either those fingerprints are already on file or when they have a suspect and they can then reinforce the case against that suspect. When you hear fingerprint evidence given you will hear of the fingerprints taken at the scene of the crime and that, at a later date, the defendant's fingerprints were taken at a police station and the two sets forwarded to a specialist officer who will tell you, in effect, that they are identical. If there is no other evidence to connect the defendant with the offence you can be sure that he has a criminal record and that he was traced through his fingerprints being on the police file. What has in reality happened is that the fingerprints found at the scene of the offence have been checked against the records and found to be those of the defendant. He has then been arrested and his fingerprints taken again and these have been compared with the suspect ones. You have been told no untruths, but not the whole of the truth, the whole object of this subterfuge being to suppress knowledge of his previous criminal record coming to the attention of the jury. A moment's thought and an understanding of the methods employed defeats that subterfuge.

A defendant can refuse to give his fingerprints to the police but a Magistrates' Court can make an order giving the police power to use force in taking the defendant's fingerprints, but this is very rarely necessary. If you hear evidence of his refusal then you can be pretty sure that, like the man who refuses to go on an identification parade, he is guilty.

The expert on the examination of fingerprints will tell you that there were sixteen ridge characteristics (at least) which were identical on the two sets of fingerprints (of any one finger(and that in his, say, ten years of experience he has never encountered such agreement between fingerprints from different people. Often there is evidence of different fingers as well: in addition it is possible to compare palmprints (footprints also) although this can only be done when the police have a suspect as there is no record kept of palmprints as there is of fingerprints. The expert can point out the ridge characteristics from enlarged photographs which are independently checked by at least two experts. Mistakes are not made. The old method, at the scene of the crime, was to dust the surfaces of articles and photograph the fingerprints which were revealed but, nowadays, the actual fingerprint impression is lifted on a plastic sheet and taken away for examination. Once on that plastic sheet it cannot be removed, so there is no way in which a fingerprint can be physically 'planted'. Many laboratories and experts have tried to do so, experimentally, but have been uniformly unsuccessful.

Identification

You can be certain that if a defendant's fingerprints are found at any particular place he has been there and, if he had no right to be there, has an explanation to give.

9

The Defendant

Now we come to the person who, in one sense, is the most important one in court, the defendant. The prosecution charges him with an offence and it is its duty to prove his guilt: never forget that. The evidence in many cases may be clear, even overwhelming, but in many the decision you will have to make will depend on the view you take of the defendant and this on the evidence he gives. It is for the prosecution to prove its case, but if, for example, when a defendant says 'I did it in self-defence', you ask yourself 'Do I believe him?' or 'Do I think he might be telling the truth?' and you answer either of those questions with 'Yes', you can not ignore the fact that the prosecution has not convinced you that he was not acting in self-defence and that your verdict has to be 'Not Guilty'.

So you try to assess the defendant. This is something which we do everyday in our ordinary lives, people we know, people we meet, but the defendant we see in unfamiliar surroundings when he is, inevitably, under great strain. How much will you learn about him to help you in making your assessment? If he is of good character or, more accurately, has no previous criminal convictions (the two things are not necessarily the same) you will inevitably hear Defence Counsel ask a police officer, 'Is it not correct that the defendant has never been convicted of any criminal offence?' There may be a rider such as '... except for an offence of driving without due care and attention' or something similarly irrelevant. If he is of good character you may hear character witnesses called on his behalf, his priest, his employer, the list of possibilities is long, but this is not very common, perhaps because so few people before juries in the Crown Court are in a position to call such evidence. You might also bear in mind how irrelevant much of this is: for example, a young curate is charged with an offence of indecent assault on a male person; of what possible value is the evidence of his bishop that he is of excellent character?; it is undoubtedly correct, but if he has any tendencies of this type his bishop would be highly unlikely to know of them. In any event, as the Judge will tell you, good character does not entitle a defendant to an acquittal – if it did no one would ever be convicted – but only to help you decide whether or not you believe what he says. As the lawyers put it, it goes to the question of his credibility: in other words you are entitled to give greater credence to a man of good character than to one who has not got that good character.

The result of the present system is that when you do not hear evidence of good character you can safely assume that the defendant has previous convictions. There are dangers here. The convictions may be for offences of a different character, perhaps unpleasant ones, and the defence feels it better, on a charge of burglary, to say nothing rather than reveal that whilst the defendant has no convictions for dishonesty he has convictions for incest. I believe that juries are only influenced in borderline cases in favour of defendants with good characters but do not allow themselves to be influenced against defendants because of their previous convictions. Much time and energy is pointlessly wasted in many criminal trials in attempting to conceal a defendant's previous convictions and even that he has any at all: by the time you have finished reading this book you will know all the signs which reveal that he has. I think that we are now intelligent and sophisticated enough to try defendants fairly even if a jury knows all about the defendant. That is the normal situation in most European countries, and courts in those countries have acquittal rates similar to our own. Character is a dangerous concept to consider in a criminal trial, especially as it is often only that of the defendant that is exposed, but you have to consider it, that is the law.

In an appropriate case you will hear the defendant tell you about his education, career and general background, this has the advantage for him as a witness of getting used to giving evidence before he comes to the main and, perhaps, difficult part of his defence. In most cases you will hear a defendant give evidence but he is under no obligation to do so, in fact, until rather less than a century ago he could not give evidence in serious criminal cases. The Criminal Evidence Act 1898 changed that and nowadays he has three options: he can give evidence as any other witness and be cross-examined by the prosecution, he can make an unsworn statement from the dock, in which event he cannot be cross-examined, or he can say nothing. Let us examine those three in turn.

(1) The defendant elects to give evidence. The defendant enters the witness-box and takes the oath or affirms in the same way as any other witness: he is a witness and his evidence must be assessed in the same way as any other witness's evidence. His counsel will, after general matters, go on to ask the defendant about the allegations against him. This can sometimes be fairly simple, sometimes very difficult, it depends on the allegations which the defendant

has to face. Take, as an example, the case of a defendant who is alleged to have wounded someone: there are a number of different possible defences. First, that although the defendant had the knife in his hand he had not intended to wound the other person, it was an accident. Secondly, that the defendant did inflict the wound but that he did it because the other person was attacking him, it was self-defence. Thirdly, that there is an error in identification and that the wound was caused by someone else. Fourthly, not only was it not caused by the defendant but that he was not even there, an alibi. The first three of these lines of defence all have one thing in common, the defendant admits that he was there, at the scene of the crime, but gives an explanation which is consistent with innocence: you will weigh up all the evidence from all the witnesses, including the defendant and any witnesses he might call, and then decide if the prosecution has proved its case to your satisfaction.

The fourth line of defence, that the defendant was not there, is generally known as an alibi: it is a word which has acquired an unsavoury meaning but, in the end, there can hardly be a better defence than to prove that a defendant was in, say, Birmingham when the offence was being committed in Southampton. Until recent years it was possible for the defence to say nothing about an alibi until the defendant went into the witness box and said, 'I was not in Southampton, I was in Birmingham.' In reality, of course, it would have become clear during the cross-examination of prosecution witnesses, in challenging identification, that the defendant was going to say that he was not at the scene of the crime, but he did not have to reveal where he says that he was at the vital time or who, if anyone, was with him at that time. Nowadays he, or his solicitor, has to give notice to the Prosecution of an alibi stating where the defendant claims he was at the time and the names and addresses of any witnesses he proposes to call to support his version. The object of this is twofold. If the police investigations support the defendant then the case against him will be dropped but, on the other hand, it may enable the prosecution to disprove the alibi evidence. A Judge may admit alibi evidence even if the notice has not been given as, for example, when the defendant purely wishes to say that he was, at the relevant time, in bed asleep. Alibi evidence then is the reverse side of the identification coin: the prosecution tries to prove the identity of the culprit, the defence raises the defence of alibi but does not have to prove it, it is for the prosecution to disprove the alibi.

One interesting feature that occurs in alibi cases is that Defence Counsel, apart from challenging the identification of the defendant, is not in a position to challenge, although he may well ask questions about, the truth of what happened at the scene. The defendant was not there so he cannot give his lawyers instructions about what happened. Defence Counsel may question the witnesses at length to try to get them to give different accounts of what happened in order to weaken the reliability which can be placed on their identifications. On the other hand, Prosecuting Counsel has little on which he can cross-examine the defendant. 'You were there, weren't you?', 'No, I wasn't' sums up the questions and answers that can be posed and responded to. Yet, despite a defendant saying he was not there, some counsel, surprisingly, cross-examine a defendant on the details of what happened at the scene and, perhaps more surprisingly, some Judges let them do so. If the prosecution is to make progress in breaking the alibi defence it is usually through the witnesses who are called to support the defendant. The defendant himself will have heard what has been said in court by the prosecution witnesses, but his witnesses will not have heard that evidence nor, indeed, that given by the defendant or any other defence witness called previously. No witness is allowed to be in court to hear evidence given by another witness until he has given his own evidence: the object of this is to prevent a witness 'tailoring' his evidence to fit what others have said previously. There is one exception to the rule in that, with the Judge's permission, an expert witness may be in the court during the giving of other evidence. Consequently, Prosecuting Counsel will cross-examine the defendant and each alibi witness closely as to the details of their evidence and, perhaps, in this way, reveal discrepancies sufficient to lead the jury to reject the alibi evidence. One of the best methods of putting forward a fraudulent defence of alibi is for the defendant and his witnesses to give evidence of an incident or incidents which did occur, so that they are all giving evidence of truth, except that it happened on a different day, for example, describing a family party which had been held on the 12 September as having been held a week later, on the 19 September. Alibis of this type are difficult to break. You will obviously be interested to know how people are able to remember what happened say six or nine months previously, and usually evidence will be given to relate the incident to a family birthday or something similar. One thing you can be certain of and that is that almost all alibi defences are false and, fortunately, will usually appear obviously so. But not all: one case on appeal from a Magistrates' Court resulted in the Judge, with two Magistrates, stating that they were completely satisfied that the defendant had been wrongly identified and that he was not at the scene, in fact it was proved that he was working underground in a coal mine at the time. Let us leave alibi cases.

In a more complicated case, such as a fraud case which has taken the prosecution several weeks, or months, to present, you will not expect the defendant to be able to deal with the allegations in a few hours: his evidence can take days and even weeks. He will have to look at the documentary exhibits and explain their significance from his point of view, perhaps giving his versions of what happened, differing from those of the prosecution witnesses, and also, even where there is agreement on facts, give his reasons for what he did which, if you accept them, give a different complexion to the nature of the acts and show that they were done innocently. In many of these fraud cases there is more than one defendant and each will give an explanation: sometimes they will blame one another so that your task can be made even more difficult. Not only will a defendant, in such a case, be a long time in giving evidence-in-chief but he will also be cross-examined at length by counsel for other defendants and by Prosecuting Counsel.

One of the peculiarities of our system is that, at least in theory, if a witness makes an averment of fact on which he is not challenged then it is assumed that the other side accepts that piece of evidence. As a result counsel often challenge every point whether of importance or not (to be fair, sometimes a point may only assume importance at a later stage), and this is, in part, caused by the interventions of some Judges when a defendant says something which contradicts unchallenged earlier prosecution evidence. Judge to counsel:

'Mr Smith. The police officer was not challenged on this?'
'No, Your Honour.'
'Well, he should have been.'

It is right that where there is a point of substance in dispute that the original witness should be challenged and given an opportunity to deal with it. The omission to do so arises from two causes. First, either the defendant has forgotten to tell his lawyers about it or counsel forgot to put it to the witness or, secondly, and very frequently, the defendant has seen the difficulty at a late stage and then denies the truth of what the prosecution witness has said. Most Judges only intervene when a point of substance has not been challenged but there are some who seem to think, like some counsel, that everything must be challenged: this is a major cause of the unnecessary length of some cases. There is one consolation to the jury: it decides what it thinks is a point of substance.

(2) The defendant does not give evidence but decides to make a statement from the dock. This is a defendant's right, a hangover from the days when he could not give evidence, but one which is under increasing criticism. It means that the defendant can stand in the dock and say what he likes without being subject to cross-examination, so that you never see him being tested. As a result, you will be told, his statement does not bear much weight as evidence on oath, but there is a lot of uncertainty as to what weight it does carry. It must have some relevance otherwise there would be no point in it and you would not be allowed to hear it. Perhaps the best way to approach the statement is to take the view that if it makes sense act on it, but treat it with great suspicion. The statement the defendant makes from the dock must be, like his evidence, his own: it must not be a statement prepared by his lawyers. It must be what he wishes to say and his lawyers can only, quite properly, draw his attention beforehand to the topics, the subjects, with which he should deal.

Why does a defendant not give evidence but make a statement which cannot be challenged? There may be situations – albeit rather unlikely – in which he does not want to be open to questioning because of matters outside the allegations which he is facing, although such questioning would usually not be allowed. He usually does not give evidence on oath because he is afraid of being exposed by cross-examination as a liar. It is the mark of the guilty man although, as the Judge will tell you, you must not hold it against a man: perhaps one day the system will also be changed.

(3) The defendant neither gives evidence on oath nor makes a statement from the dock. The reasons for this are the same as where he does make a statement from the dock but, at least, it has the merit of not telling lies. It can also come about in the case where the defendant has told his lawyers, 'Yes, I did it but I'm not going to plead guilty, let them try to prove it.' This a defendant has the right to do but it means that counsel cannot ask any questions which suggest that the defendant did not commit the offence and, of course, it would be impossible for the defendant to give evidence.

There is one last situation which you may encounter, where the defendant is unrepresented and conducts his own defence. This is something he has a right to do except that a court can, apparently, refuse to let him dispense with the services of lawyers in the middle of the case. The unrepresented defendant is the dread of most Judges and Prosecuting Counsel. Quite understandably, the defendant does not know the rules and there can be a lot of confusion, in addition to which most Judges feel that they have to go out of their way to see that the defendant's interests are protected. To be fair, though, there are occasions when unrepresented defendants have done as well as if they had been represented as, at least where the defendant is reasonably intelligent, his knowledge of the facts of the case may outweigh his lack of knowledge of the law.

10

In the Absence of the Jury

In Chapter 5 we looked at a situation where the jury is asked to leave court whilst counsel is trying to persuade the Judge that a witness's original statement can be put to him because he has turned hostile. This is only necessary when a party wishes to discredit his own witness: the other side can always put an earlier statement to a witness. This is, however, not the only situation in which a jury may be asked to leave the court and, in fact, is not the most frequent nor the most important reason for it being requested to do so. The Judge is the judge of the law, the jury are the judges of the facts.

A major question of law is whether or not the evidence is admissible: there are many rules on that question. The first rule is whether the evidence is relevant and, usually, counsel, either alone or in consultation with his opponent, appreciates the relevance of the evidence, or otherwise, and only relevant evidence is introduced. If there is any dispute about relevance the Judge will decide. What is meant by relevant? Broadly, does the evidence go to prove, or disprove, anything at issue in the case: there are exceptions to the rule which, of itself, does not prove any fact in the case. The second rule is, even though the evidence is relevant, has it been properly obtained? If there is any dispute between counsel as to relevance or the defence is objecting to the admissibility of any evidence on any other ground then it is for the Judge to decide. It is then quite understandable that the Jury leaves the court during the discussion otherwise they would hear the evidence which is the subject of the argument that they should not hear it! Let us though look at the two major reasons for juries being asked to retire.

The first is the question of the defendant's character to which we have already referred: you will note how the question of character may, at least in the eyes of the lawyers, come to dominate a trial. If he has a good character you will hear about it fast enough. But if he has a bad character, that is to say previous convictions, he does not need to tell you about them nor can the prosecution introduce evidence about them nor cross-examine him about them except in certain circumstances, and then only with the leave of the Judge. Sometimes the character of a defendant slips in by accident, for example, when a prosecution witness says, 'I met him in Wormwood Scrubs when we were doing time together', in which event the defence may apply for a fresh trial and, usually, in blatant circumstances like those the Judge will grant the application, but not always. The application to a Judge to put a defendant's character to him will arise usually where in the course of cross-examination of defence witnesses, one or more of them is accused of lying or that witness's own criminal convictions are put to him. Incidentally, you can get another clue to whether or not a defendant has a bad character if Defence Counsel attacks a prosecution witness in that way when the Judge, as he is supposed to, draws Defence Counsel's attention to the dangers of the course he is taking. So, if at that stage, the Judge says, 'Mr Brown, you know where this may lead', or something similar, you will know that the defendant has previous convictions, possibly serious or numerous, or both. Very unusual, but equally proper, if a man of bad character gives evidence that he is of good character the prosecution can ask the Judge for leave to cross-examine him on his record. The reason for allowing a defendant to have his bad character put before a jury is that the jury has a right to know, to enable it better to assess the relative truthfulness of a witness and the defendant, the true facts about both their characters and where the witness is alleged to be lying, even if he is of hitherto good character, the true nature of the person accusing him of lying.

For a long time lawyers thought that a defendant's character only 'went in', to use lawyers' jargon, when either he attacked the character of a witness or accused him of lying other than in the case itself, in other words if he said that the witness was lying and that the lies related to the case and it was a necessary part of his defence it did not 'put in' his character. The House of Lords, as the supreme appeal court, put an end to that idea and it is equally open to 'put in' a defendant's character when his defence essentially requires the allegation of lying. Thus a defendant who alleges that a prosecution witness is lying is in great danger of his previous convictions going before a jury. You will remember that the object of you knowing about a defendant's character and previous convictions is so that you can assess his credibility: what reliance can you put on his word? Be careful though: you will hear details of his convictions, Borstal for burglary, prison for wounding, and so on. You must not say to yourself, 'He's done burglaries before so he's just done one more.' Although common sense tells you that he has most likely done it this time if he has done it before, it does not follow. It might be better if, when a Judge decides that a defendant's character should be admitted, the jury were just told, 'This defendant has been convicted of criminal offences in the past. This does not prove he has committed this offence any more than good character would prove he has not committed the offence. You must consider this information only to help you decide on his credibility.'

Whilst you are out of court Prosecuting Counsel will draw the Judge's attention to the attack on the prosecution witnesses and ask for leave to cross-examine the defendant on his character. Defence Counsel may try to argue that the attack was not such as to permit the prosecution to follow this course or, more likely, will argue that the Judge should exercise his discretion and not allow the cross-examination to take place as the prejudice which might arise would so outweigh the probative value (why that phrase is used I do not know as the bad character of the defendant has no probative value, as the Judge will tell you). Judges' attitudes vary from those who virtually always admit cross-examination to those who do not like the House of Lords ruling and exercise their discretion in favour of the defence. You will be able to recognize that this is going on as it will occur when the defendant is being cross-examined and usually after Prosecuting Counsel has asked him questions about the facts of the case and then accused him of lying: this is considered to be the correct tactical moment to attack his character, after the attack on his truthfulness, as if to say to the Jury, 'You've heard what he has said but now you know that he is a man of bad character so you can discount his story.' Much of the effect of this is lost because of the break caused by the jury having had to leave the court. When you return to court either everyone will pretend that there has been no break, in which case you will know that the Judge has exercised his discretion to keep the defendant's character 'out,' or you will hear of the previous convictions: either way you know he has some.

The second major reason for you being asked to leave the court will occur much earlier in the trial, during the course of the police evidence. When dealing with the opening of the case by Prosecuting Counsel (Chapter 4) I mentioned that one should listen carefully to check if he did not tell you anything about any conversation between the defendant and the police or, more often, about any statement made by the defendant. Of course, if you are told that he made no statement that is that: it is when nothing is said that you should be on the alert. The point at which you will be asked to leave court will most likely be when the first police officer reaches the point of interviewing the defendant at the police station. The objection to the admissibility of evidence of what passed between the defendant and the police officers applies equally to oral and written statements but I will deal with the written ones first.

You will hear something like this: 'I then spoke to the defendant at the interview room at the Central Police Station. I cautioned him [this is the piece where the defendant is told that he need not say anything unless he wishes to do so but that anything he does say may be taken down in writing and given in evidence] and asked him ...' If the oral part of the evidence is not objected to, on the ground of admissibility, then it will be given: this does not mean that it is accepted by the defendant as being true nor that it is true. But then, just before the officer says, 'I said to him, "Do you want to make a statement?" ' (the details of which the Judge and the lawyers will have in the files of statements before them, but which you will not have), Defence Counsel will be on his feet with an interjection such as, 'Your Honour, there is a point of law which arises at this point.' You will now know, without possibility of error, that the defendant made a statement of admission (if it were not damaging to him he would not be

107

challenging its admissibility) and that he is now denying that he made it voluntarily. The jury will now leave the court and the police officer will resume his evidence in front of the Judge, counsel and the defendant, giving the defendant's answer to his invitation to make a statement.

'He said, "Yes."
'I said, "Shall I write it down or will you?"
'He said, "Will you?"
'I then took down the statement, Exhibit 14.'

Prosecution Counsel will question the officer carefully so as to establish the words recorded in the statement were the defendant's, that no pressure or threats were used and that the defendant freely made it and signed it. If the objection to the admissibility extends to the conversation alleged to have taken place between the police officers and the defendant than a similar proceeding will take place in the absence of the jury. This proceeding, like that on the admissibility of a statement, goes only to its admissibility, not as to its truth.

If a defendant, when the charges are put to him in court, says, 'Guilty', you might think that is the strongest proof of his guilt. He does it openly, is represented by lawyers and is, one assumes, aware of what he is doing. A not quite so good, but acceptable, method of proof is where a witness tells you that the defendant admitted to him that he was guilty, or admitted facts from which you can arrive at the decision that he is guilty. Of course, on most occasions where a defendant has done that he will plead guilty. The jury, though, will only be concerned with situations when the defendant is alleged to have made a statement of admission but, despite that, has pleaded not guilty. What then is the basis upon which a court, a Judge, admits as evidence a statement alleged to have been made by a defendant? It must be voluntary: he must not have been forced, threatened, coerced, persuaded, tricked or promised any advantage to obtain the statement. Whether the statement is true, or not, is irrelevant, so a truthful statement which is not voluntary is not admissible. The rule is carried to its limit in that Prosecution Counsel is not permitted to ask the defendant if it is true until, and unless, the Judge admits it into evidence. There have been cases where a man, who was obviously guilty, admitted the offence to the police in writing but has been acquitted on the Judge's direction (or had his conviction quashed on appeal) because there has been no other sufficient evidence than the inadmissible statement. So what is happening in court whilst you are out?

Prosecution Counsel will continue his examination of the police officer who produces the statement. He will then be cross-examined by Defence Counsel to put to him the allegations which the defendant makes about his treatment by the police. The range of allegations made can be very wide. They are almost always untrue, very rarely they are true: sometimes there is some element of truth in the allegations, a slight irregularity which is exaggerated. An allegation against the police of physical violence is rare, that is, to allege that the defendant was beaten until he signed a confession: for that to happen it would require the co-operation of a number of police officers and, in addition, the defendant would bear the marks of the violence. Even if there were police officers willing to do that they would realize the inherent dangers in doing so. Coercion or threats, for example, telling the defendant that if he does not confess to this offence they will see he is charged with others, are two irregularities more often complained of by defendants. Persuasion can be brought to bear by telling the defendant that if he makes a statement confessing to the offence the police officer will speak up for him in court but if he does not make a statement, then ... Threats, coercion and persuasion may overlap. It would be unrealistic not to accept that these things do happen, or combinations of them, even though they may be borderline cases. In any event, at this stage, you do not have to make a decision, that is the task of the Judge. A more subtle allegation sometimes made is that, although the defendant made a statement and signed a statement, the document which he signed does not contain what he told the police: in other words the police officer taking down the statement has written down a confession which the defendant has not made. This means that it is not his statement and, if the allegation is true, can not be evidence against the defendant. After the cross-examination of the police officer who produces the statements other police officers may be called, either who were present when the statement was taken or who are in a position to negative allegations put to the first police officer about police behaviour in general relating to the defendant; they will also be cross-examined.

It is then open to the defendant to give evidence before the Judge and to call witnesses. There is very rarely any point in this: if there is any real chance of keeping the statement out of evidence then, if Defence Counsel has not achieved a breakthrough in cross-examination, the evidence of the defendant is unlikely to convince the Judge although, sometimes, combined with other evidence (such as physical injury) it might. Very few statements are excluded by Judges. Whether this is due, as some believe, to the average Judge being pro-police and anti-defendant, or to the fact that it is rare that statements are obtained improperly, is a matter for debate. In the case you are hearing you, as jurors, can decide for yourselves whether or not you believe the statement is a voluntary one because, when the Judge has decided that the statement is, in his opinion, voluntary, and thus, admissible, you will hear the police officers give evidence as they did before the Judge in your absence.

Counsel sometimes do not formally challenge the admissibility of the statement in the absence of the jury but launch their attacks on the police evidence for the first time in the presence of the jury as many counsel believe, with some Judges with good reason, that they will not succeed in keeping the statement out so that, rather than give the police a trial run in the absence of the jury, they will do it when they are unprepared. If that course is followed then you will have heard Prosecuting Counsel tell you about the statement in his opening address to you.

Once the statement has been ruled as admissible by the Judge you have to accept it as evidence in the case; you can not decide that it is inadmissible and ignore it if you come to the conclusion that it is not a voluntary statement. What you can do is to accept the defendant's version that it is, for example, not his statement, and your approach to the credibility of the police officers' evidence in general will be affected by your conclusions as to their behaviour. On the other hand, and this is much more likely, to be the situation, if you believe that the allegations against the police are wholly unwarranted, you may not only accept the statement as clear evidence of guilt, but it also gives you invaluable guidance as to the character of the defendant.

What sort of evidence given by police officers in relation to statements made by and challenged by defendants should you treat with some suspicion? There are two types which you should examine very closely. First, where a defendant's statement contains items which incriminate him but which are not supported by any other evidence: this does not mean that they are not true and voluntary but examine them carefully. Secondly, when a police officer does nothing else in the case except take the statement and the defendant is alleging pressure on him by the police but not by that officer. It is then not open to the defence to develop its argument by cross-examining the officers who are alleged to have put pressure on the defendant: so be a little suspicious if the prosecution does not call those officers.

A similar situation affecting the defendant is where the statement which he is challenging was made in the presence of his solicitor and that solicitor is not called to support his version. You can be quite sure that the solicitor, as you would expect, is not prepared to support the defendant's lies.

One question you may be asking after you have returned to court is, 'Why did it take so long?' Apart from long-windedness of some barristers, and Judges, and the fact that many witnesses may have had to be called, the English system of criminal justice has some built-in factors which tend to lengthen proceedings. First, unlike most (if not all) European countries, England does not have a criminal code where all the law concerning crime is collected together, so often time is lost looking up the law. Secondly, the provisions of the law have to be considered by the courts, particularly the Court of Appeal, and interpreted and these cases are reported in series of Law Reports, of which there are too many. So, if a point of law has to be argued counsel may have to refer to a number of legal authorities, in different sets of Law Reports, and they may not be exactly on the point which is before the Judge so that analogies have to be drawn between the various cases. In addition to all these questions of admitting evidence, the Judge has a discretion to exclude evidence which is prejudicial. This means that whilst the evidence is technically admissible, the Judge is of the opinion that its prejudicial effect is greater than its probative value: for example, evidence of a defendant having taken drink but not being drunk. Argument by counsel on this can take considerable time.

11

The Jury's Rights

In the Preface I said that 'courts do not tell jurors what is going on all the time, sometimes from oversight, sometimes deliberately.' In fact, no courts tell juries about some of their rights, and two of them are of great importance.

The first is the jury's right to ask questions. It would be unfair and myopic not to recognize why courts do not tell juries about this right, but if the reasons for not doing so are good ones then it would be better for the jury to have that right taken away from it: in fact, its exercise by juries might have a refreshing effect on an almost frozen system. You will be told by the Judge, at a very late stage in the trial, that you are the judges of fact, he of the law, and this is perhaps a useful division which can be made in relation to questions. A jury's questions, which should be put by the foreman, can be directed at two recipients, the Judge and the witness. The major difficulty which arises is that a jury only really gets together to discuss the case when the Judge has completed his summing-up, when it is too late to ask any questions of witnesses, although the jury can ask the Judge to clarify his summing-up of the evidence.

How then to go about asking a question? The jury, or any

member of it, should wait until counsel have completed their questioning and then should direct their questions to the Judge, for example, 'We would like to know if the light was on' or 'Who reported the incident to the police?' Fortunately most, if not all, of the relevant questions you will want answered will have been asked of witnesses by counsel but not always, so do not be afraid to do so. However, do not do it just for its own sake, cases are already overlong, but do not be put off by the Judge: he can, of course, prevent you asking questions of a witness of a type which could not be put by counsel or himself, because they are not relevant and/or admissible. In other words, your questions must conform with the rules, that is why it is wiser that you should put your questions through the Judge. For example, you must not ask questions about people's characters: if no one has done it already it is because it is inadmissible, in any event you will already have a good idea about the defendant's character without anyone mentioning it directly.

The right to ask questions is an important one, and it is not infrequent that juries ask Judges for help after they have retired to consider their verdict, only to be told that there is no evidence about the matter and that, then, it is too late to call any. Therefore, before the end of the evidence you should ask your questions, or if you want to, for example, see the car in the case, or the place where the incident occurred, say it early on: you are the judges of fact and have a right to know; exercise that right when you think it is necessary. Incidentally, Judges are reluctant to order visits to the scene of the crime, but particularly in cases of street fighting (affrays and riots), they are very valuable: the scene looks very different from the plans and the photographs you may have been shown in court. If you come up against a Judge who refuses you your rights the temptation may be great to say to yourself, 'I'll teach him a lesson and acquit the defendant.' Do not do that, it would be wrong, although in some cases the lack of the information you are seeking may make it impossible for you to decide the case so that you will be compelled to acquit the defendant: the end result would be the same, but the justification would be legitimate, not based on pique.

The second important right a jury has is to stop a case at the end of the prosecution case. Judges do not normally tell you that, in fact only extremely rarely, and counsel are not allowed to tell you: a strange right you have which you are not allowed to be told about! At the end of the prosecution evidence a Judge can stop a case if the evidence, even if all believed, does not establish the allegations in law: this is his duty and the jury plays no real part in it. The Judge can also stop a case if it is so weak, or the evidence so unreliable, that in his opinion no reasonable jury could convict on the evidence: alternatively, he may invite the jury to consider it at that stage. If he does that you can not come to the decision, at that stage, that the defendant is guilty (even if you think so), only that either you want the case stopped and the defendant, as a consequence, acquitted, or that you want it to proceed in the normal way. However, even if the Judge does not tell you that you can stop it, you can do so, but only after all members of the jury are agreed on that course of action. If you want to discuss it with other members of the jury you should tell the Judge that you wish to do so and ask his leave to retire to the jury room.

Surprisingly, Judges and juries disagree more often, though not publicly, in cases where the Judge wishes to stop a case and a jury does not! This is not unusual with some Judges, who are trying unnecessarily complicated and tedious fraud cases which they, like everyone else, are having difficulty understanding and are dreading

117

the thought of having to sum-up, decide that the easy way out is to listen to legal argument by counsel, in the absence of the jury, and stop the case. In that event you will be brought back into court and the Clerk of the Court will say to you, usually after the Judge has explained to you his decision, 'On His Honour's direction do you find the defendant not guilty of ...' If, on the other hand, he invites you to consider whether or not you wish to stop the case, it is in your hands to do so or otherwise. If the Judge tells you that, in law, there is no case to answer you have no option but to return a verdict of not guilty. The disagreement between Judges and juries I referred to above may come about when a jury cannot follow the convoluted legal reasons for a Judge stopping a case: if that is so then they should ask for explanation. However, if the Judge says to you that the evidence is so weak that you ought to acquit the defendant the temptation to disagree may be great and, if that temptation is genuinely supported by your convictions, would not be wrong. Remember on the law you must follow the Judge's instructions, on the facts you follow your own conscience and judgement. There is a third right which a jury has which we will see in its correct place in Chapter 13.

12

Speeches
and Summing-Up

When all the evidence has been given it then falls to
counsel to address you. Prosecuting Counsel first, then
Defence Counsel: if more than one Defence Counsel, then
in the order in which the defendants they represent are in
the indictment. You will be relieved to know that where a
defendant is represented by two counsel only one of them
will address you! Some counsel are mercifully short, others
tediously repetitive: one always remembers the latter.
What, though, is the object of the exercise? What will
counsel be attempting to achieve in their addresses? You
heard Prosecuting Counsel, when he opened his case, tell
you what he hoped to prove but now you have heard the
actual evidence and you may think it desirable that the
Prosecution should now tell you its attitude towards the
case. Even more so that Defence Counsel should wish to
interpret the evidence in a way which is most favourable to
their clients.

Prosecution Counsel will attempt to relate the evidence
which you have heard to the various allegations against the
defendant, to urge you to accept some particular piece of
evidence given by one or other witness and reject that given
by the defendant and his witnesses on that same point. His

duty is to try to show you what the issues are and on what evidence the prosecution relies. Defence Counsel will, understandably, refer you to evidence which supports his client's case, again urging you to accept the defendant's evidence and to reject that of prosecution witnesses, and will attempt to show that the prosecution has not proved its case. It is where there is more than one defendant that the complications develop, when, for example, the defendants disagree or one blames the other for committing the offence.

Speeches are often long, sometimes lasting hours, even days in long fraud cases and yet even counsel wonder whether they achieve anything. After six or seven days of speeches by Prosecution and Defence Counsel a jury goes out to consider its verdict and returns with it within a couple of hours: has the jury been helped by the speeches? That is, at least, one question that you will be able to answer after you have heard the speeches. One thing to look for in a speech by Prosecuting Counsel is whether he really deals with and defines the issues and tells you of the evidence in support of each of those issues or whether he devotes himself to a wide-ranging attack on the defendant: the first is helpful, the second not so.

When listening to a speech by Defence Counsel, again, ask yourself is he dealing with the evidence or does he restrict himself to criticizing Prosecuting Counsel's speech or talk in generalities such as the burden of proof, the wonderful legal system we have, how the jury system is admired world-wide, or, in identity cases, does he speak a long time about all the cases in history, long past, where there have been miscarriages of justice: these are all signs that he cannot think of anything to say on the facts, in other words he thinks the defence case is hopeless: you might think that an interesting sign! It is the one way in which you might discover the opinion of counsel, for he is not supposed to express his own opinion to you. As a result you will hear counsel use such stilted phrases as 'You might think, Members of the Jury ...' or 'It might be thought ...', not 'It is my opinion ...' or 'I think ...' The reason for this is that it is only the jury who are allowed to express their opinion of the evidence when they return a verdict of guilty or not guilty.

Advocacy is an art which is practised not only in the courts but by, amongst others, preachers, politicians and salesmen. It is the art of trying to convince the listener that the speaker's point of view is correct, that his is the way to salvation, that the political theory he is propagating will save the nation, that the motor car he is trying to sell you is the best. Many of these people, one hopes most, believe in what they are advocating: there have been many cases, though, where people have definitely not believed what they have been advocating and, perhaps more dangerously, those who have genuinely believed in a false religious creed, a harmful political belief or in the virtues of a worthless article which they are trying to sell. The difference in the case of counsel is that he may, or may not, believe in that which he is advocating and that it is quite irrelevant whether or not he does believe it. It may be said, on the one hand, that it is a most immoral act to attempt to advocate something in which one does not believe but court advocacy can be considered to be in a slightly unusual position. Defence Counsel is using his ability, his training and his experience to put before a jury the defendant's case in a way which the defendant himself would put it if he had that ability, training and experience. That can perhaps be countered by asking if that is not as bad, or worse, than arguing a false case on one's own behalf. This is a moral question difficult of answer and fortunately, as jurors, you do not have to do so.

You may wonder why it is not possible for Prosecuting and Defence Counsel to be able to agree what differences exist between the prosecution and defence cases and address you only on those. In reality, the differences between the two versions may be very small, if important, for example who struck the first blow, but in deciding that question you may have to consider many other disputes, as to who started the argument, what was the true relationship between the injured man and the defendant's girlfriend, so that counsel will be addressing you not so much as to 'who struck the first blow' but on all the surrounding circumstances and the background. Generally speaking most counsel try to keep to the point, some succeed, some do not and some do not appreciate, or appear to appreciate, the point as clearly as others do. What is genuinely inexcusable is the failure of counsel to face up to the case which his client has to meet and, as bad, are the interminable speeches and continual repetition.

When counsel have completed their speeches the Judge will sum-up the case to you. He will tell you that his summing-up will have two parts to it, law and fact: that he will tell you what the law is and you must accept that from him and, if he is wrong, the Court of Appeal, in the event of a conviction, can put him right, but that the facts are for you, and you alone, to decide. First, the law: he will tell you it is for the prosecution to prove the case against the defendant, what it has to prove to establish the various charges against the defendant and will deal with the law, where it is appropriate, on such matters as character, alibi and identification. This part must be attended to with great care because you have to act on it: you will usually not find it too difficult to follow as experienced Judges know how to explain it clearly. If there is one fault that some Judges have it is to repeat themselves, to try to explain the same point of law in different ways, which can lead to confusion. The more difficult part is the evidence. It is on the evidence which you have heard that you decide what facts are proved and, then, if those facts provide the proper basis to prove the allegations against the defendant, you will find him guilty, if not, then not guilty.

The form of the summing-up will usually remain the same, law, then fact, but the amount of time spent on the facts will naturally vary according to the amount of evidence which has been given. A trial in which the evidence has taken only a few hours should not take long to sum-up, whilst one which has lasted for several months may well take many days to complete. But, however long or short the summing-up takes, remember it is being done by the Judge to refresh your memories of the evidence given or, at least, of that which he considers relevant. If you do not agree that he has dealt with all that you consider relevant then you act on what you think is relevant: many, perhaps most, Judges will tell you to do just that. You may also form a view of the Judge's opinions; if you agree with them follow them, if you do not ignore them: again most, if not all, Judges will tell you to do that. Some Judges will tell you that they have not formed opinions on the evidence: this is difficult to believe, but whether it is true or not, you ignore other people's opinions, such as those of friends or relatives who during the course of the trial may try to discuss the matter with you, other than those of your fellow jurors, when you discuss the verdict.

After dealing with the law the Judge will spend most of his time dealing with those parts of the evidence which are in dispute whilst only dealing in outline with those parts which are agreed. There are two basic methods used by

Judges in reminding you of the facts. One is for the Judge to go through the evidence in the order in which it was given, at the same time pointing out its relevance to the case which the defendant faces. This is quite helpful in a short case, or where the disputes are simple, and means that you are reminded of all the prosecution evidence first and then the defence evidence. It has not been unknown for a Judge at the end of a long case to go through the evidence, as his own note records it, in full; on one occasion a Judge covered some fifteen days evidence in one day reading at great, and almost unintelligible, speed. Another Judge used to remind the jury of the defence evidence first, then the prosecution, giving the impression that the burden of proof had been changed as well as putting the prosecution case more firmly and prominently in the jury's mind.

Perhaps the best way for a Judge to sum-up is to tell the jury first that certain matters are not in dispute and then deal, in order, with those which are in dispute, giving the prosecution evidence and defence evidence in relation to each dispute separately. That this is seldom done is because it requires a lot of work. You will have noticed, during the trial, that the Judge has been keeping a note. This is to help him in summing-up the case to you, but it has two main disadvantages: it can lead a Judge to concentrate too much on the note to the neglect of controlling his court and if any important piece of evidence is omitted from the note it will also be omitted from the summing-up. It is difficult to know how summings-up, in general, can be improved so as to be more helpful to juries; perhaps the best way will be to find ways of shortening cases. A Judge's task is not an easy one as many, particularly the High Court Judges, have much else to do out of court, and the easy way of reducing the burden is to sum-up by going through the note from beginning to end.

Speeches and Summing-Up

You have by now heard speeches and summing-up and instead of having been helped you may be more puzzled than ever. If the case is clear that will be due more to a good summing-up than anything else but do not allow yourself to be swayed by it. Do not forget, you decide.

13

Deliberation and Verdict

The decision over guilt or innocence you will come to in
your retiring room and this is, in one sense, the one field in
which the lawyer can do little to help you. Officially no one
knows what goes on in the jury room, as jurors are not
supposed to tell anyone what happens in there but,
surprisingly, jurors are not sworn to secrecy, the oath that
is taken by each juror does not include any such
commitment: the only intimation of this restriction comes
in a notice in the jury room. It is however an ages' old
tradition, and one which is generally respected and a
breach of which can be dealt with by the Court as a
contempt, so it is wiser to say nothing about what went on
in the jury room. One of the results of this is that we know
very little of what goes on in there, or in the minds of
jurors. Judges and lawyers can not be certain whether or
not the approaches they adopt are ones which help juries,
or, particularly in the case of the advocate, whether they
appeal to them. Perhaps it is just as well in some respects
otherwise even more time might be wasted than at present.

One instruction you will be given by the Judge is that
when you retire to your room you should elect a foreman
(foreperson) to preside over your discussions. Such an

election is usually by secret ballot, by show of hands or, perhaps, by general acclamation. In many ways it would be better if the jury were to elect a foreman at the opening of the trial. This would enable two things to be done which are virtually impossible at the end of a trial. First, you would have a spokesman to raise questions with the Judge during the course of the case and, secondly, someone to lead discussion during the course of the case, which leads me to a reform which I think would be desirable. That is that, in long cases, juries should have time to discuss the case as it proceeds, if they so wish. This reform would require no legislation, it only needs a jury to tell the Judge that they wish to retire to discuss matters amongst themselves. Having done so, they could, through their foreman, pose any questions they wish and, if in any doubt or confusion, ask for guidance as to what is going on.

Who do you elect as your foreman? You will have had enough trouble trying to assess the character of the defendant and the various witnesses without trying to do the same for the other eleven members of the jury, in order to decide the most suitable person to be the foreman. Be a little careful about selecting the strongest personality, you are not electing a leader but a chairman, a person who will lead the discussion, not dominate it. It can be very easy for a strong personality, foreman or otherwise, to dictate to the rest of the jury. Do not allow that to happen to you. Listen to argument, be ready to change your mind if you are persuaded by argument but otherwise stick to your own point of view, that is why you are there. If you are convinced of the defendant's guilt, even if the others are not, stick to a guilty verdict: if you are not so convinced, then 'not guilty'.

Before you retire to consider your verdict the Judge will give you a direction about majority verdicts. Until recent years, a jury had to be unanimous in finding a verdict, all twelve for guilty or all twelve for not guilty. If that could not be achieved then a re-trial had to be held. It is the practice that if a second jury cannot agree then the charges are dropped: there is no third trial. There then came a point where it was at least suspected that juries were being interfered with, that is in certain major criminal trials friends of the defendant would bribe or threaten a juror into refusing to convict. If this was done at both trials the defendant escaped justice. It was thought that if majority verdicts were introduced, as they were in the Criminal Justice Act, 1967, whereby a verdict of ten to two could be accepted (either for guilty or not guilty) it would require three jurors to be bribed or threatened, in each trial, into voting not guilty. It may well have been successful in preventing interference with juries, but it is surprising how often juries still cannot come to a decision even on a ten to two vote. If, as a juror, you are approached by anyone during the course of the trial who attempts to influence your verdict you should immediately report it to the Clerk of the Court or to any other officer of the Crown Court: they will take all the necessary steps.

The Judge will tell you, when you first retire, to try to be unanimous, and only after you have had a considerable time to consider it will he be prepared to accept a majority verdict. He will also tell you that when that time comes, if it is necessary, you will be brought back to court to be given instructions on majority verdicts. The law lays down that a minimum of two hours should pass before a jury can be given the majority verdict direction: in fact, Judges allow at least an extra ten minutes to be on the safe side and, in long complicated cases, may well wait for five or more hours before giving the direction. On return to court for such a direction the Clerk of the Court will ask the foreman, in respect of each count in the indictment, if you have agreed on your verdict. It may be that you have agreed on some counts in which case you will be asked to give your verdicts. The Judge will then tell you, in respect of all the counts on which you have not agreed, that he will now accept verdicts of ten to two: you will then retire again to your room. Sometimes it still takes a long time to reach a decision on that basis: sometimes it is still impossible. It may be that you cannot remember a particular piece of evidence whilst discussing the matter or you want further guidance on the law: if you do you can return to Court and ask the Judge for his help. Having agreed amongst yourselves on majority verdicts you will again return to court where the Clerk of Court will again ask you if you are agreed on your verdicts, that is on verdicts on which at least ten of you are agreed: the foreman must answer that question simply with a 'Yes' or 'No'. He will then be asked what, in relation to each count, that verdict is. If the verdict is 'Not Guilty' he will not be asked, and must not say, whether or not it is unanimous or by a majority, but if it is 'Guilty', he will be asked if it is unanimous or by a majority and, if by a majority, whether it was eleven to one or ten or two.

One word of warning: do not allow the concept of majority verdicts to affect your own personal decision on the way in which you vote. What if you cannot agree on the basis of a majority vote? If after trying as best you can then the only thing which can be done is to return to court and tell the Judge that agreement is impossible: the degree of division, for example, six to six, must not be revealed. If this happens the Judge will discharge you from returning verdicts and the case will have to be retried before another jury.

How do you go about the task of deciding? In a simple case it is a good idea to take a vote straight away, particularly in a case which looks obvious: of course it might not appear obvious to everyone on the jury! In a longer, more difficult case the whole issue may still revolve around whether the defendant is honest or not: if so, decide that first, then all else will fall into place. On the other hand, you may have to decide a number of different issues, in which case it will be best to deal with each in turn before moving on to the next. Is the dispute whether or not the defendant admitted his guilt to the police? He has challenged that: who do you believe? Your decision is a very serious act. By that act you may condemn a man or woman, so you must think deeply and carefully but you must not be unprepared to return a verdict of guilty, however unpleasant that may be. One thing you must never do is to compromise because it is expedient: not to say 'Well, the others think he is guilty and it is rather late' and then say 'Guilty' when you do not think so. It might not be so bad if the compromise on grounds of expediency results in an acquittal, but never against a defendant.

You may, on the evidence, be forced to convict a defendant although you may all feel that, whilst he has done wrong, his wrongdoing was understandable: his personal and family circumstances and the background to the offence make you feel that guilty he may be but that he should be more moderately punished than would be normal. It is open to a jury, on finding a defendant guilty, to add a rider to that verdict recommending that he should be treated mercifully. No one will tell you that, Judges do not, Defence Counsel is not allowed to do so. So you have another right about which you are not told. Do not do it lightly; perhaps not surprisingly, in cases where juries do make recommendations for mercy, the Judge usually takes the same view in any event.

When you have delivered your verdict your task is over. Sentencing is the Judge's responsibility. Normally you will remain in court while this is done but, sometimes, particularly at the end of a long case, and even more so when there are three or four defendants, the Judge may defer sentence until the following day. If you do remain the first thing that you will hear is Prosecuting Counsel calling a police officer who will produce to the court the defendant's 'antecedents'. These will give personal details, such as age, education, marital status, work record, financial position and previous convictions. The officer may be asked questions by Defence Counsel but after a bitterly fought case, where the police have been attacked, he is unlikely to get much said by the police officer which is favourable to the defendent. The next step will normally be the production of a report made by a probation officer: this will be longer and more detailed than the police report (which is usually purely factual) and will go into the defendant's character in greater detail. Some are full of utter humbug but good probation officers produce reports which are valuable to the courts in deciding sentences. There may also be medical reports, especially psychiatric ones, all of which are intended to help the Judge in deciding the correct sentence. A Judge has to weigh the seriousness of the offence, the defendant's propensity for crime, the future opportunities for the defendant and the interests of society. The last step before sentence is for Defence Counsel to address the Judge in mitigation of sentence and he will attempt to present all the favourable features, if any, revealed either in the evidence or in the reports presented at the end of the case: some of these speeches affect Judge's sentence, some are really proforma and have no effect on the sentence, and indeed are delivered with no great expectation of having any effect.

Sentences are pronounced by some Judges with long moral homilies. I doubt if many convicted persons are in a state to benefit much from these homilies at that stage. In recent years sentences have become much shorter than they used to be. There appear to be two main reasons for this: first, there is now great doubt as to the effectiveness of long sentences and, secondly, the prisons are overcrowded so pressure has been put on Judges to reduce the length of sentences. The danger here is that too much leniency may discourage the police from chasing criminals. After a two-year fraud investigation by two detectives working full-time, and after a six-week case, one defendant received a six-month prison sentence and the other a similar sentence, but suspended: the detectives were visibly discouraged.

Often at the end of long or difficult cases Judges make orders excusing jurors from jury service either for life or for a stated number of years. This can be of great value to some jurors, particularly those with their own businesses as jury service can be a recurring duty.

14

Reflections

Undoubtedly when the trial is over and either the defendant leaves the court a free man or the Judge has sentenced him, you will in the days and weeks after your jury service think about what you had been doing in the Crown Court. Your prime thoughts may be, as they must be with many, why was it necessary to waste so much time and money over the trial of a man who was so obviously guilty? Why, and how, is it possible that one guilty man can cause so much trouble and cost? It is true that only two types of defendant can afford long trials, those who have unlimited private means (they do not seem to get involved in long criminal cases!) or those who have nothing and thus receive legal aid without paying any contribution or, at least, only a very small one. It is an instinctive reaction to say, 'Stop it!' But how? The task of the jury is to decide whether or not the defendant is guilty: it would not be possible, or proper, for anyone else, Judge or lawyer, to look at the case in advance and say, 'He has a defence which might be believed', so he gets legal aid, or, 'There is no believable defence', so he gets legal aid only if he pleads guilty. Such a decision would have to be made on the basis of paper evidence only, the depositions and statements, and by now you will have seen that the only way you can really decide is by hearing the witnesses. That is not the way out. Legal aid has come to stay and without it the vast majority of defendants would be unrepresented. If time and money are to be saved and at the same time trials made easier for Juries to follow, a few reforms are needed.

It might be that the whole method of trial which we have is antiquated. There is a basic difference between the Anglo-Saxon system, as used in England, the United States, Australia and other countries where English legal influence has been dominant, and that based originally on the Roman Law, but owing more to Napoleonic reforms, as in France, Italy, Spain, Germany and the other West European countries. Scotland is a hybrid. The Scottish legal system owes much to Roman and Roman-Dutch law but has many of the features of the English system with trial on indictment (known as Solemn Jurisdiction) before a Judge and a jury of fifteen. The jury has always been able to return verdicts by majorities, not only of 'guilty' and 'not guilty', but also of 'non proven' where the jury is not certain of guilt or innocence. The system differs in other ways in that, for example, there is no opening address and Scottish Judges appear to be able to sum-up trials much more concisely than their English brethren but, despite that, the Scottish juror, as well as those in Anglo-Saxon jurisdictions other than England, will undoubtedly, during the course of trials in which they are participating, be able to recognize similarities with the English trial. It is not, as is often thought, that in England a defendant is innocent until he is proved guilty whilst in, say, France he is guilty until he proves his innocence: that is just arrant nonsense, no democracy would tolerate it. Not only is it not true of the democracies but neither is it true of countries behind the Iron Curtain: their government have no interest in the conviction of innocent people in ordinary criminal cases.

Reflections

The essential difference between the two systems is that in England the prosecution makes an allegation against a defendant and has the duty of proving it without being able to insist on the defendant giving evidence. In most Continental countries the defendant is interrogated by an Examining Magistrate in the preliminary proceedings and is called to give evidence at the trial. The differences are often summed-up by two phrases, English as the 'accusatory system', the Continental as the 'inquisitorial system'.

The object of court proceedings is to achieve justice, the essential requirement for justice to be done is for the court to know the truth. Some features of the English system are designed to prevent the truth being revealed, often for understandable technical reasons due to the strict separation of the functions of Judge and jury, whilst the inquisitorial system aims, I stress aims, at the truth. The Continental lawyer can see no reason why the defendant should not be obliged to give evidence. To introduce that into England would be a major step and perhaps not acceptable: the furthest that most lawyers will go is that a jury should be allowed to take a defendant's failure to give evidence into account when deciding his innocence or guilt. (Legislation along these lines is in hand at the time of writing.) It has always been thought wrong that a man should contribute to his own conviction by giving evidence: why? Justice should be a concept above that of the State or the individual and, providing no improper pressure is used, any steps taken to arrive at the truth should not only be acceptable, but also demanded.

The object should be justice based on truth, the maximum that can be obtained relating to the allegations made against a defendant presented in as clear and concise a form as possible. What prevents that being achieved? We have looked at the problem of the defendant not giving evidence and, as a change there seems likely to be

137

unacceptable, let us concentrate on the two major obstacles. First, the failure to present concrete issues before a jury and, secondly, and to a great extent caused by the first, overlong speeches and summings-up.

Let us look at the failure to present concrete issues to the jury. The courts of England do not concern themselves only with criminal cases: there are, all the time, disputes in civil matters, heard by a Judge without a jury, disputes over contracts, or allegations arising out of, for example, road accidents or industrial injuries. In those cases the plaintiff makes an allegation against a defendant and has to present 'pleadings', in effect making the allegations which he will rely on at the trial: the defendant then has to either admit or deny each of the allegations in the pleadings. It is not quite as simple as this but at least by the time the trial starts the Judge, who will have read the pleadings, will know what the issues are: for example, although there may be a dispute as to who is responsible for a road accident, both sides may agree the injuries and damage to the vehicles, so that it is not necessary to call witnesses to prove those matters. Why it is not possible to introduce a similar system into the Crown Court is a mystery: perhaps only inbred lethargy can explain it. If such a system were introduced, you as a juror would hear, at the beginning of the case, that the defendant was charged with handling stolen property, that he pleads not guilty to the charge but that he admits certain facts, for example, that he bought the car from a named person, that he now accepts that the car was stolen, but denies that he knew it was stolen when he bought it. In a serious fraud case it might be that most of the facts revealed by hundreds of documents could be reduced to a few pages of agreed facts and then you would only have to hear evidence on the matters in dispute and the defendant, perhaps, explaining that when he did something it was done innocently. This system would have the enormous advantages of, first, concentrating the mind of the prosecution on what it has to prove, secondly, enabling the defence to tie the defendant down to his real defence and, thirdly, enabling the Judge to know, with much greater certainty, what he is trying. I do not doubt that properly operated such a system would cut court time, *in toto*, by as much as half.

Even if such a system could not be introduced, not because it would be difficult to operate but because the political will to introduce it does not exist, another reform would be to limit the time counsel have to address juries. Perhaps openings of over half an hour should be banned except where the case is complicated and the Judge gives leave: in such cases Prosecuting Counsel would be required to have his opening speech written down and submitted to the Judge. In fact, if it was insisted that opening speeches were all written down in advance they would be better and shorter. Closing speeches could also be restricted in length in the same way. Changes of this sort would also meet with great resistance as the members of the Bar have always prided themselves, perhaps not unfairly, on their ability to perform their tasks orally and have never liked the idea, which exists in some American jurisdictions, of what are called legal briefs, or written legal submissions. One bad point, though, about the English system is that it is time-consuming. There could be no reason why these reforms should not be introduced along with those of written pleadings. I am convinced that such changes would revolutionize the English courts without in any way altering the burden of proof or taking away any of the existing safeguards which try to ensure that no innocent man is convicted.

This book, though, has not been written with a view to reforming the law but, it is hoped, to help jurors understand better what is going on in court, and why. If it has done that, its main purpose has been achieved: if, in addition, it has awakened an interest in the reform of the law, then that is a bonus.

Index

Page numbers indicate where substantial discussion begins